Living in Faith Everyday

Sociology through Religion

with Mindful Daily Living Stories

Dr. Yunus Kumek

Sage Chronicle
publishing house

Cover images and interior images selected by T. Hajdaj from Pixabay

Sage Chronicle $^\lambda$
publishing house
www.sagechronicle.org
3380 Sheridan Drive, #240
New York 14226
contact@sagechronicle.org

Copyright © 2020 by Sage Chronicle$^\lambda$ Publishing House

ISBN 978-1-951050-08-5

All rights reserved. No part of this publication may be reproduced, stored in a retrieval system, or transmitted, in any form or by any means, electronic, mechanical, photocopying, recording, or otherwise, without the prior written permission of the copyright owner.

Published in the United States of America.

CONTENTS

Preface ix

Defining Religion and Understanding the Scientific
   Approach Behind It 1
     Cosmology through Religion *1*
        The Ant *5*

Religion, Its Definition and Sociology 5
     Dedication of All Acts to None but God *5*
        The Ant and the Carpet *6*
     Positive Group Associations *7*
     Humans at the Center of Creation *8*

Secularized Life, Science, and Religion 8
        Head of the State & The Poor Man *10*
     Sample, Analysis, and Results *12*

Human and Self in Religion 13
     Primary Life: Soul *13*
     Self: Tool of Realization *14*
     Secondary Life with Revelation *15*
     The Most Holy Spirit and Jesus *16*
     The Greatest Name *17*

Goal, Meaning, and Purpose in Religion 18
     Belief and Disbelief *18*
     Difficulties and Problems of the Method of Comparison
        in Knowing God *20*
        Meeting after Years *23*
     Value of Human Being *23*
     Psychological Example of Disbelief and Belief *27*

    The Realities, Our Weaknesses, and Our Short Life............29
    Belief and Excellence *30*
    True Belief and Spreading Religion. *30*
    Order, Chaos, and Meanings. *31*
    Prioritization *32*
        Out of Trouble Man and Marriage in Heaven................**32**

Deity, Humans, and the Religion 33
    Existence and Non-Exist. *33*
    The Purpose of the Scriptures Related to Present Christianity,
        Islam, Judaism, Buddhism, and Hinduism *34*
    Localized and Boost Treatment *35*
        The Health of Faith & Practice............................**38**
    Human Language, Reductionism, and the Role of the Scholars. *39*
    Peaceful States of Heart. *40*
        Silence, Smile & Peace....................................**41**

Social Constructs and Religion..................................... 42
    Normalizing the Human Reality. *42*
        Cat Hanging around with Humans.........................**44**
    Normalizing the Mistakes *45*
        Going Back and Back **45**
    Manifestations and Reflections of Names and Attributes of God. *46*
    Embodiment of Supplication. *48*
    Human Value Systems as Social Constructs *48*
    Golden Rules to Remember. *50*
    Claims of Self or Nature-Related Existence *50*
        Worldly & Spiritual-Seeming Achievements & Fatalities **53**
    The Obsession with Impossible Statistical Arguments. *54*
    The Word 'Nature' as a Social Construct *58*

Epistemology of Religion.. 63
    Realms in Religion. *63*
        Trials & Tests **64**
    Personal Choices *65*
    Religion and Western Philosophy *65*
    Method of Religion. *78*
        Owner's Manual...**80**
        Loud and Silent **82**

Effects of the Society and Humanness 84
The External, The Internal, and the Purpose..................90
Religious Symbolism and Conflicts...............................*91*
Inter- and Intra-Religious and Non-Religious Group Interactions
and Conflicts *91*

Conflicts Due to Diseases of the Heart 92
The Internal Enemy...*92*
How to Cope with Envy...*92*
Winners and Losers..**95**
The Stains of the Heart and Chest *97*
Distorted—The World of Filthy Self...............................*99*
Heart Diseases and Detection **100**
Different Worlds of Ego and Heart...............................*101*
Expectations, Disappointments, and the Formation of Physiological or
Psychological Sickness...*102*
Lies and Show Off *106*
Killing as an Outcome of Spiritual Disease *106*
Phrases on the Tongue **109**
Observation and Analysis..*110*
Method of Learning...*112*
Etiquette and Morals of Learning.................................*114*
Learning with the Children **115**
Etiquette and Morals as Reminders of our Limits..................*115*

Attitudes, Behavior, and Religion................................. 117
The Process of Formation of Doubts..............................*117*
Reliance of God **117**
Attitudes Leading to Belief or Disbelief *118*

Religious Attitude, and Behavior 120
The Real Achievement..*120*
The Real Embarrassment..*122*
The Embodiment of Modesty *123*

Change and Religious Adaptation 123
Victories and Openings after Being Patient.......................*124*
Imbibing Patience **126**
The Path of God—Stability......................................*127*

Religion in the Lives of Individuals 130
    Theodicy..*130*
        The Lost Phone..**132**
    Etiquette and Morals with God *133*
    Death and Theodicy..*134*
    Scriptures as a Blessed Inductive Guidance *134*
    Prophets, Messengers, and Role Models as the Practical Source
        of Guidance *142*
    Relationship with the Scripture and Prophets: Reminders *142*
    Prayers, Alienation, and Theodicy *143*
        Pain in the Eye & The Prayer **144**

Rituals as Collective and Social Engagements 144
    Collective Rituals...*144*
    Company of Religious, Ethical, and Good People *145*
    Rituals in Representation of Divine Authority.......................*145*

Rituals as a Source of Solidarity 146
    Religion and Globalization *146*
    Apocalyptic Unification and Conflicts *152*
        Signs & the Earthquake..**155**
    Layered Authority: Checks and Balances between
        Governments and Religion......................................*155*
    Abrahamic Religions and Special Commonalities...................*158*

Being Religious and Spiritual 159
    Negligence..*159*
        One Hand, One Leg, One Eye **159**
    Gratitude *163*
    Spirituality: Focusing on the Heart, Emotions, Experience,
        and the Self *163*

Conversion.. 165
    The Real and Pseudo Self...*165*
        Galxies and the Person **171**
    Self and the Divine..*172*
    Change and Reversion or Conversion *174*

Contents

Self-Accountability and Religion 174
    True Sanctification with the Prophets 174
    Falsehood in Self Sanctification and Following the Devil 175
        Dual Identities 176
        Spiritual States and Baklava 177

Collective-Social Accountability and Religion 178
    Certainty in Afterlife 178
    No Doubt in Afterlife 179
    The Purpose of Punishment, Hell, or Accountability 181
    Manifestations of Wisdom and Power: This Life and Afterlife 184
    Afterlife in Detail 184
    Explicit Arrogance: Historical Disease 188
    Inductive Knowledge and Explicit Punishment 188

Religion, Experience, and Emotions 189
    The Concern for Ending and Locating Different Emotions 189
        Two Cases 191
    Heaven and Merit and Compassion of God 193
    Emotional Memories 195
        The Reality of Missing 197
    Hope and Fear: Heaven and Hell 198
    Realities of Fear, Death, and Hope 199
        Communication with the Unknowns and Unseen 200
    Negativity and Faith 201
    Meaning, Purpose, and Religious Actions 202
    Patience and Reliance (Trust) 202
        The Professor 203
    Happiness 204
    Now I Have Understood! 206

Reality of Emotions and Experience in the Relations with the Divine ... 207
    Religion and Migration-Diaspora 207
        The Teacher and Humbleness 209
    Innate Potential Powers of Humans 212
    Breaking the Natural Divine Promise 212
    Middle Way 213
        The Spiritual and the Semi-Buddhist Spiritual 214
        An Argument at the Temple 251

Acknowledgments... *217*

Author Bio.. *219*

Index *221*

Bibliography *223*

PREFACE

There are two perspectives to understand: the interaction between the religion and sociology. One is to give an understanding of sociology, community and group from the perspective of religious scholarship. The other is to give an understanding of religion from the perspective of the established methods of sociology with its theories and methodological frameworks. The goal is to develop our own critical thinking through the merger of these two perspectives.

To accomplish this, one can read this textbook to review the approaches of understanding sociology through the established perspectives and methodology of religion. Therefore, the title of this book is "Sociology through Religion."

Then, one can review the religion through the perspectives and established methodology of sociology. One can find classical textbooks titled as "Sociology of Religion" referring to the social and group dynamics of religion through the theories and methods of sociology.

Finally, one can then try to combine both frameworks of sociology through religion and religion through sociology in order to form one's own critical understanding and analysis for the interaction between the two.

Therefore, this textbook is highly recommended to be used as a supplementary textbook along with the traditional textbooks of sociology of religion. The instructors, who really emphasize critical thinking with different frameworks, will find a high value in this book to be used as a textbook along with other books in the fields of sociology and other social sciences.

Yunus Kumek, PhD
Harvard Divinity School
Lecturer, Spring 2021

This book is an extended version of "Sociology through Religion" with additional practical stories. The stories can help the readers to realize the relevancy of religion in the everyday life of a person in different social, kinship, professional, and communal engagements.

A Religious Person in Social Life

A religious person can view the world, the universe, personal and social encounters in relation to their primary meaning and purpose with God, Adonai, the One, Nirvana, Karma, Intelligent Design, Allah or other names that can be implicitly and explicitly uttered.

A religious person can try to deduce courage with a meaning from this perspective. A person is expected to not be scared of anything except God. When people are all panicking because of disasters, evil-seeming misfortunes, the religious person smiles and knows that everything works with and in the Name of God. If God does not allow or permit, not a single thing can come into existence even before it occurs in our realm.

A religious person gains wisdom from everything [1]. A religious person learns from his or her mistakes. A religious person learns from an animal. A religious person learns from the plants. A believer builds upon their certainty in the divine reality when studying the physical wonders of the creation surrounding them. From physics, mathematics, geography, oceanology, and other areas, science readily strengthens the faith of a believer and connection to their Lord. All of this knowledge for him or her has relevance, purpose, and meaning on the path of God.

On the other hand, a person who is a lost wanderer is always in chaos. They overlook profound meanings in smaller things in life. A light breeze comes, they swing in one direction. Another breeze comes, they swing in another direction. A lost wanderer does not have a foundation. Therefore, they "go with the flow." A person who is a lost wanderer ignores their spiritual self. They just consider the physical body as the self. They are always in fear, anxiety, and stress. If a disease comes, they panic. If some misfortune befalls them, they fill with anger and resentment for reasons that are unexplainable in this world. The wanderer lives a life of randomness

A true religious person lives a life of amazement and pleasure in this life. A true religious person driven towards the admittance of their soul into the real pleasure of this existence; an eternal existence in a paradise awaiting, independent of this quick "pitstop" one calls "life". They can feel as though they are in Part II of the same movie of amazing pleasure.

For the true religious person, Part I contains the pleasures and amazements in this world and Part II contains the pleasures and amazements of the next life after death.

Cat and Mouse

Piper had a cat in her house. Her cat's name was Saber. One day, Saber found a mouse at home and started chasing it. The mouse went into a hole. Saber went outside the hole and waited there patiently until the next day when the mouse came out. Piper was watching this and was amazed with her cat's patience. She acknowledged Saber as one of her teachers in learning patience.

IN PRACTICE

In religious practice, it is very important to observe everything—the animals, the objects, the plants, and the changes. Active and critical thinking is an expected methodology to increase one's knowledge on the spiritual path. The knowledge is useless unless the person benefits himself or herself.

© Pixabay

Defining Religion and Understanding the Scientific Approach Behind It

Cosmology through Religion

One should understand that there is a fine line between the will of God and a person's intention, inclination, and effort towards achieving something in this life. For example, if a person had an intention to hurt someone with a gun and then takes the gun to shoot someone, the effect of this shooting on the other individual is dictated by God. The person has the free will to do good or bad but there is an accountability for this person in the world and in the afterlife. In this case of shooting, the person is blamed who performed this evil. If God did not create the effects of the means and reasons, then there would not be the concept of free will or free choice in good or bad. The people will not get or achieve what they desire to achieve.

On the other hand, God limits the extent of evil that humans potentially give and receive due to divine mercy. These ways of God can be mystical, unknown for most people but not for a select group of people close to God. In this reality, if a person is protected from evil engagements in one's life, it is truly due to the graciousness and mercy of God. A tiny portion of this effort, maybe as an intention or inclination, can be credited to the person. Conversely, if evil befalls a person, the person should look at his or her own free choice or free will in unconsciously desiring the occurrence of this evil. In some cases, the evil-seeming incidents can hit the person without his or her control. This may have another perspective to elevate one's level in one's relation to God. In other words, it could be a recall message to go back to God and establish a positive relationship with the Creator.

In another perspective, there is the full willpower of God. God created humans with a microscopic willpower accompanied by free will and free choice in their short life spans. Humans' willpower is so small that there are discussions among scholars if it should be called intention or inclination of the person rather than willpower. In this perspective, the person intends and inclines towards an action, then God makes and creates the intended action for the free choice of the human being. In this sense, the creator of this action is God, but the one who made the choice is the person. So, the person cannot blame anyone but oneself in dealing with a bad outcome of an action.

In addition, the action emerges in the world of ours, when God's infinite willpower coincides with the tiny willpower of the creation. Most of the time God does not allow evil to emerge due to divine mercy. But the person keeps asking and struggling for the outcome of this evil. Then, at this time, due to this person's free will and choice, God creates this action. On the other hand, God gives mercy without the person deserving it. For example, creation from nothing, seeing, hearing, eating, tasting, religion, and guidance are all due and from the mercy of God.

Another important methodology in Divine Creed is that knowledge follows the already known. In other words, when someone knows something, it is a discovery of a reality that is already there. If the person does not know or discover something, the reality is still there. Therefore, the title of this book is knowing and discovering what is already there. The authors and the people's discovery do not make a change to the reality of the Scriptures. Similarly, God created humans so that they can discover and learn about Him and the wonders of His creation. Through analysis and synthesizing, a person can bring to light an infinite number of realizations that had always existed before their knowledge of it. In short, there is no invention but only discovery.

Therefore, humans' knowledge does not add anything but the effort of discovery. Through critical thinking, analysis, and rationality, these discoveries can take place. We can call this science today. We did not create 'Conservation of Energy' in physics, it had long existed before it was discovered by science. God made it. We discovered it. We are using it in different applications of engineering. Then, we can call this theoretical science, knowing the conservation of energy. Applying this discovery, on an appliance such as a refrigerator can be called applied science. We are using and synthesizing what is already there.

Finally, knowing God truly can allude to this fact, as God is always present. Humans' true knowledge of God is the purpose of creation. The positive sciences are the steps to serve this goal of knowing the Creator, the One, God. If a person does not know God truly then it does not change anything about the reality but offers a miserable and incorrect rendering of the meanings and purpose in life and in the afterlife. If a person knows God, it changes everything and offers a happy and true rendering of the meanings and purpose in this life and in the afterlife.

The infinite knowledge of God can also be referred to as fate or destiny. The Divine Knowledge about the outcomes does not make the person void of their responsibility of free will and free choice.

The isolation from religion due to sins is a process, not a one-day or instant event. If a person can think of the scientific process of rusting, it requires time for the chemical reaction to happen. This rusting and detachment occur as a process due to the choices and actions of the person. In this regard, free will is the person's acquirement and no one can blame God that the choice of disbelief or misguidance was a force or compulsion. It is interesting to note that one of the ways to prevent rusting is painting. If the sins are like rust and painting can be seeking forgiveness, then refreshment of religion will occur through seeking forgiveness, knowledge, and worship.

When the person sins and then seeks forgiveness, the person may still feel remorse or regret in his or her heart although the person seeks forgiveness. This is a good sign because the ability to differentiate right from wrong is still present in the person. If the person does not seek forgiveness, the person can lose this ability over time.

When the person's choice coincides with the God's Will, then the action happens immediately. In this perspective, God does not make evil or prevent people from wrong belief. Conversely, many times God gives time to the person who intends evil. God does not create the evil action that the person has been constantly seeking. But when the person continues to seek, finally God allows the formation of this evil. After, God creates what this person intends as this person demands it with free choice.

On the other hand, for the good, again this person desires it to happen. Then, God helps and gives blessings in this person's renderings in this world and in the afterlife. Even if the person may not achieve what he or she wanted, God still rewards this person according to his or her intention.

In other words, religion is the core, pure, and genuine asset of the person. When the person does not recognize God, there is some harmful radiation that can come from the heart of the person which can be deadly for others. God seals their hearts in order to protect others.

THE ANT

There was an ant who was going on pilgrimage. Hudson saw him and engaged him:

Hudson: Where are you going?

Ant: To the holy sites.

Hudson laughs, and says: I do not think you will make it. The holy sites are a thousand miles away from where we are right now.

Ant: I know that, but I have the intention.

Hudson feels so ashamed about the ant's answer and declares the ant to be his teacher.

IN PRACTICE

Intentions precede actions. If a person intends always for the good and beneficial, God rewards the person according to the person's intention. If a person prays or gives charity to the poor with the intention of showing off to people or to gain some worldly benefit, the person can get what she or he wants in the world, the tag. After death, the person can be punished due to not acting sincerely. Also, in practice, religious people commonly observe nature, animals, and plants and try to learn from them to increase their spiritual development.

Religion, Its Definition and Sociology

Dedication of All Acts to None but God

The true worship of God should be given and instructed as an inductive teaching by God to humans. The inductive teachings should be by God. Worship should be given as an inductive, top-down approach of revelation to humans. Humans can approximate meanings about God. Yet, these are all approximations unless these approximations are confirmed with the true and absolute knowledge of revelation from God as an inductive teaching.

Limited humans cannot claim to know about God, who is transcendent and beyond human beings' limited approximations. Knowing something can mean comprehending and surrounding that thing mentally by intellect, logic, and mind. Yet, limited humans cannot know truly about God, who is transcendent, unlimited, and infinite unless with the permissibility of this true knowledge given by God.

The main creed about God cannot be based on secondary, mystical, or interpretative meanings that can lead people to illusionary and unstable discourses of skepticism, agnosticism, spirituality or others. Yet, there are pillars of the religion such as the knowledge about true worship which should be on clear and simple pillars. This knowledge should be referenced to the clear inductive teachings of revelation as instructed by God.

THE ANT AND THE CARPET

Peyton was in the temple. She saw an ant walking on the carpet. The carpet was nice and green with some designs. Peyton said to herself, "Wow! This ant probably thinks that he is in a green ocean."

IN PRACTICE

In the above story, the ant was on a two-dimensional plane compared to Peyton who was on a three-dimensional plane and can therefore see the design of the carpet. Peyton was above the carpet, looking down. In practice, it is understood and experienced that there can be millions of dimensions. Some mystics can experience some of them.

Similarly, the knowledge and experiences of the Transcendent, the High, God can sometimes be simplified and reduced to the human understandings of time and space. One should not forget that the similarities do not give the person the essence about the Divine. There is always room for error. Therefore, caution with possibilities and the statement of "God knows best" is added in internal and external expressions.

Positive Group Associations

At the end of the day, there will be group associations. Yet, a believer of God and the follower of prophets of religion should clearly mention their disposition at one point but not cross the boundaries of positive group identities of a believer. This occurs especially when people approach everything with possibilities, agnosticism, skepticism or recent illusionary approaches of religion or cultural appropriations. In this regard, there is an implicit hit on the positive group associations of being religious as the follower of prophets on the path of God by expanding the popular negative discourses against the institutionalized religions.

Humans at the Center of Creation

Humans are the center of all creation. The purpose of the universe and the existence of other creation is humans. There has always been an emphasis on humans and their relationship with God since the time of the creation.

With the narrative of Satan, there is a creature working against our purpose on Earth which is to worship God. Therefore, we should not forget the reality of temptation and our egos, as instigated by Satan with an incalculable amount of tricks.

The only way to be safe is to accept our own weakness in all of our life philosophies take refuge in God. It is imperative that we take refuge in God for protection against Satan, yet we are negligent.

One should really understand our limits in that we are the creation and God has the authority, discretion, and preference of whatever or however to implement according to the divine will. We do not have any power as miniscule beings. This is a reality. This may not be emphasized in our Western discourses due to the self imposed problems of alienation from God. Yet, it is a reality for a person to adjust one's respectful attitudes, etiquette, and morals with God.

Secularized Life, Science, and Religion

When we review the immediate accessible content of the Scriptures, one can realize that implementation of justice in personal and social lives and, accordingly, accountability and afterlife is a major theme in the scriptures.

In this regard, other topics related to science serve to support the primary accessible and immediate apparent content.

The content of science in the Scriptures has a value when it is attributed to God [2]. Magnifying or idolizing science without any reference point to God induces partnership. Yet, this is contradicting the purpose and goal of the Scriptures.

In this regard, one of the critiqued points of problematic separation in religion all over the world is that it introduces science as a new deity or god without explicit religious language. This adoration causes new emerging groups such as scientology, etc. to use this available market of accessibility in the secular societies.

In other words, one can understand the reasons for separation of church and state to increase accessibility for everyone without mentioning the name of God due to different understandings of religion and religious practices. Yet, referring to it with uncommon or unpopular non-religious language such as nature, science, or others induces adoration to these implicit deities followed by submission.

For example, when a person is sick and wants to be treated, he or she may say, "I want to be treated with whatever science (medicine) says." Then, the person submits to this abstract notion. Yet, true critical thinking and scientific knowledge requires not blind submission. Science is a virtual concept. It is the humans' understanding of the world through their minds with trial and errors and recommended solutions.

In the above case, the doctors treating or dealing with this case can instruct the patient in their consent forms that they, the doctors, are simply trying to do their best but there are a lot of things beyond their control and that anything can happen. At the end, they can have a successful recovery or in another possible scenario, the patient may even die.

At this point, the person who idolizes science dives into huge disappointments of unknowns, uncertainty, depression, fear, and anxiety with unexpected results in this treatment. There is nothing that can soothe him or her, not even science or the people such as doctors who personified this knowledge. They, doctors, themselves are openly and clearly mentioning their limits as humans to protect themselves from any type of malpractice. In this case, the person puts all the burden of these fears and uncertainties on his or her weak shoulders. Before surgery, this patient already feels so much spiritual weakness and death.

On the other hand, a person of religion knows from the beginning until the end of this process that science is only the means. Doctors are only the means. The person follows medical steps to fulfill the means as made available through the laws of God in the world as part of the laws of God.

Yet, this person does not give importance to these means, but relies on God and says, "Oh God, I know You don't need these means to cure me. Yet, I do it to respect your principles and laws as instructed to us by the prophets."

Then, the person takes all of the burden from his or her weak shoulders as the patient and relies on God for all of these unknowns, uncertainties, and possible errors, mistakes or side effects as mentioned in the consent form.

HEAD OF THE STATE & THE POOR MAN

There was a poor man in the temple suffering from paranoia. Every day, he used to come to Knox in the temple and tell him how everyone is planning against him in the temple. One day, as usual, this poor man came to Knox in the temple. He said to him, "Were you here when the head of the state came yesterday? He came here to plot against me with others in the temple. I am a citizen of this country. They cannot kick me out." Knox did not say anything as usual and offered him a coffee.

IN PRACTICE

Sometimes, our ungrounded fears about others overwhelm us and make us dysfunctional. If this happens constantly, then it can become an illness referred to as persecution complex or paranoia which can lead to psychosis. Yet, it is important to diagnose it in its early stages before it becomes an illness. On the spiritual path, having a good spiritual teacher, a good collective meditation group, a good friend, and daily regular personal spiritual practices can be some of the means to detect and remove the seeds of these diseases before they grow further. Reliance on God constantly, removing and discharging oneself from all fears and anxieties with this chant, and regular daily prayers can be some of the practical remedies that can prevent building plaque on the heart and mind causing emotional and mental disorders.

Sample, Analysis, and Results

To prove the existence of anything there should be evidence indicating the existence of it. For example, if someone claims that there was someone in the house, then the house should show evidence of a change, movement, or indication to prove the claim.

In this sense, we are immersed in the signs of the existence of God. In other words, claiming otherwise will require closing one's eyes, blindness, or purposeful stubborn ignorance and negligence.

In this regard, these signs are referred to as verses in the Scriptures. All of our experiences of life are different verses and signs. All of nature is a verse and sign. All of science is a verse and sign. All of the disciplines of science are verses and signs. All of our social interactions, kinship relations, and time and space are verses and signs for the existence of God.

In this perspective, all of the signs lead to amazements of God's existence and knowledge referred to as intuitive knowledge. All of the engagements of science along with fascinating discoveries and inventions have lead to amazements of God's existence and knowledge referred to as intuitive knowledge.

In this regard, analyzing the evidence referred to as science or scientific discoveries but not taking the next step of critical thinking leading to evaluation, results, and conclusions does not befit the scientific methodology of critical thinking and evaluation.

In a good academic research article, the result and conclusion of the analysis should be supported by the entire article. In other words, the evidential result and conclusion should be mentioned in the entire article through the support of the critical analysis of the sample, pieces, cases, and data. In this sense, sample or data serves for the evidence of the proof of the claim or conclusion.

In this sense, data is a vehicle to prove the theory or the scientific law. There can be a million sets of data to prove the same theory or scientific law. In this regard, data is secondary compared to its leading results and conclusion.

Similarly, some of the content of the Scriptures is focused primarily on the results of the oneness of God [3], and accountability requiring justice and prophetship compared to the secondary content of the applications or data from which these results are acquired.

In other words, nature and science as the laws of God, can all be secondary to serve the real purpose of the primary content.

In that sense, if one considers an abstract of a long article, it is worded in a few lines mentioning the data and methodology leading to results and conclusion.

Therefore, in an article, if the author mentions constantly the data without indication of analysis leading to the results and conclusion, then this article would not be considered a scholarly well-written study. The reviewers will consider this as a case of mere reporting without any analysis.

Similarly, if the Scriptures mentioned something about nature and science, then the data would be present without analysis. With the favor and mercy of God making the test of this life easy on us, the entire body of Scripture strongly and consistently presents the primary and conclusive results- such as the oneness of God, accountability, justice, and authentic knowledge and instruction through scriptures and prophets.

The Scriptures miraculously make the primary meanings accessible for all readers through a chapter, a verse, a word, and even a letter. At the same time, the Scriptures open different doors for different seekers in different disciplines. One can find similar miraculous renderings in the hadith (sayings) of the prophets.

Human and Self in Religion

Primary Life: Soul

In its primary meaning, one can find the meaning of the life that is given to us initially by God as being the primary realization of the person's being with his or her life as given and bestowed by God.

The bodily engagements such as the organs, eyes, or hearing are all dependent on existence but not primary. There is no meaning of a body without life even though the body may be still intact with all of its organs such as the eyes or ears.

In this context, one can consider and remember the funeral scenes of a full, intact corpse of a human body without life. Although there is the full body, people rush to 'get rid of it' meaning that they do not believe that this body has the same full features of a living human. Therefore, this body should no longer belong to the social life of living humans although a few minutes or hours ago, this body was talking to them before it was dead.

All of these discussions prove that the primary and essence of what we call or define as 'human' is the thing that gives life to it. This thing in terminology is referred in the Scriptures as the 'soul'.

Self: Tool of Realization

After this primary self-realization of existence referred to as the soul is existent and given the primary condition of being a human, then the body can be considered to serve as a tool or vehicle.

On another note, one may refer to this self-realization as 'self'. Self is expected to realize one's own existence and one's own life referred to as their 'soul'.

In this regard, all of the beings that we see and realize in the universe as animals, plants, animate or inanimate beings are in full realization of their existence. Therefore, they show gratitude and appreciation to God in different forms of prayers.

At this point, what differentiates humans and other Spirits from everything is their additional given tool. This is called free will and free decision making.

Yet, this additional bonus 'million dollars' or 'fortune' can cause a lot of humans and other Spirits to become arrogant and heedless due to their additional fortune or wealth. Then, the person can choose to follow the path of disbelief. Due to arrogance, he or she may may become egoistically motivated to the point of claiming his or her own self as their own deity, as Satan did.

Or he or she may become so vainly driven as to claim his or her own identity implicitly from other Spirits like Satan did in the presence of God. In this sense, these humans and other Spirits go to the lowest of ranking among all beings such as animals, animated, or unanimated beings.

On the other hand, this additional bonus 'million dollars' or 'fortune' can make some realize that this fortune is bestowed by God, aided through their own self-realization and existence. This realization can lead them to humbleness and humility to the oneness of God. Due to this humbleness and humility towards all of the bounties of God, then they try to embody gratitude to God. This embodiment of gratitude can be called thankfulness to the Creator. In this position of the "realization of self", the person now tries to actualize this submission to God with their free will and free choice with the graciousness and mercy of God. In this regard, one can see the epitome of worship through the prophets who even surpassed all the beings including the angels.

One should realize that with this primary condition of life or existence referred to as the soul, then self is the realization of this life and existence.

Secondary Life with Revelation

With the graciousness and Mercy of God, God bestowed on us the revelation, the Divine Guidance through the scriptures and prophets in order to help us truly realize the existence of our own life and to not be sidetracked by the additional 'million dollar' bonus given to humans referred to as free will or free choice with the highs of arrogance or false self-identity claims.

In this regard, all the scriptures and prophets sent by God are another form of life that help us truly realize the real meaning of our life and the purpose of existence.

Today, the Scriptures and the practice of the prophets is the life to revive the dead and the sick souls in order to give them the true meaning of their own purpose, existence, and life.

The Most Holy Spirit and Jesus

One can now understand the technical term of 'The Most Holy Spirit' given as a title to the angel Gabriel. Gabriel has brought the revelation to all of the prophets. In this sense, revelation is the life given to humans by God as delivered by Gabriel.

In this sense of engaging with the beings of God, the Scriptures are the source of life. Gabriel is the blessed and noble deliverer of the life of revelation. All of the prophets of God engaging as the receivers of the life of revelation can also give life to us.

Yet, religions fall into the mistake of distancing themselves from the oneness of God with the trinity in their misunderstanding of The Most Holy Spirit as the Deliverer of the Life and receiver of this life from The Most Holy Spirit. Gabriel is like other angels in his position with God.

They forget the laws of God. Whoever engages with the spirits of these sources of life, they can get some type of life in different quantities and qualities. Yet even this engagement is done with wrong intentions. However, they may still receive the effect of life from them. According to the Scriptures, there are the traces of Gabriel, The Most Holy Spirit. A rebellious follower of Moses took some traces after he left and tried to give life to a calf. Then, the calf showed some type of life symptoms. Even, the traces of the spirit of the Blessed Delivery of Life, Gabriel as the Most Holy Spirit, can have an effect.

Yet, people forget and make the mistake of mixing the projection or reflection with the essence. God is the Only, One, True, Absolute Source.

The Most Holy Spirit and all of the prophets including Jesus are the blessed and noble spirits of the delivery of this life from God.

In this sense, Jesus also has the direct relation with the Deliverer of Life, Gabriel, The Most Holy Spirit through his mother, the Blessed Virgin Mary.

Therefore, due to this special position of being in the effect of The Most Holy Spirit, Gabriel, he can have similar traces of life with the permission and enablement of God.

In this regard, one can review this wrong rendering of trinity deviating from pure monotheism, oneness of God with the wrong renderings of giving deity to Gabriel the Holy Spirit with his engagements of life, and Jesus due to his performed miracles.

One should remember that everything occurs with the enablement and permission of God. Gabriel is a Blessed servant of God and Jesus is a Blessed servant of God.

The Greatest Name

The high level of Gabriel among other angels referred to as the Soul or The Most Holy Spirit is due to Gabriel's relation with one of The Greatest Names of God as the Everlasting, that is the Source of Life and Existence.

In that sense, one can interpret the relation of Jesus and Adam with The Greatest Name of God, the Everlasting. It can be due to this relation of Adam with this The Greatest Name that he is the most inclusive prophet as the father of all humans representing life in population and multiplicity. It can be again due to this relation to Jesus with this The Greatest Name that religious people are in high numbers today and until the Day of Judgment that they would be in multiplicity. The prophet Muhammad unites as the final and all-inclusive prophet of God according to Muslims.

The prophets have the relation with the Name of God as the Most Loving, therefore, the title of the prophets is the Most Loved, and therefore, God put the love in creation for this community. Therefore, this community is the best community among all as the prophets have the highest position with God as the Most Loved.

The prophets have the relation with the Name of God as The All Merciful, therefore, the Scriptures mention that the prophets are for the good of all humans.

The prophets have the relation with the Names of God as compassionate and merciful, therefore, the Scriptures mention that the prophets are compassionate and merciful for all creations.

Goal, Meaning, and Purpose in Religion

Belief and Disbelief

In religions, the importance of knowing that a person lives a short life and accordingly taking advantage of this life is very critical.

Belief is a light that is the outcome of a humble acceptance and confirmation of all the *required* parts of the religion in its *details,* brought by the prophets. Everyone has a different level of understanding and education. Therefore, a person's inability to express the intrinsic, exact notions of belief does not mean that this person does not have access to or ability to possess a belief. Most of the time, language is insufficient to describe the fine details of one's emotions and beliefs in one's heart and conscience. Even, there are many outstanding experts and scholars in textual and literary fields, however they may even lack the ability to express some of the finer details in a convoluted piece of a poem. In this perspective, if a person asks a non-formally educated farmer or a villager a question such as, "Which direction is God in?" and they answer, "God is not in any direction, it is not possible," then this can be a proof of belief in this person's conscience that God is not bound to any direction. But this inability of expression does not mean that he or she does not have belief.

According to Taftazani [4], belief is a light given from God to the person's heart due to the person's intention of seeking. Then, the person has a meaning and purpose in relevance to the entire creation and universe in the person's relation with God. They are all servants and creations of the Creator. With this perspective, the person feels secure, safe, and affinity with everything. With this power of belief in the heart and mind, the person can have resistance and stamina in the face of all evil-seeming incidents, trials, and tests. This person knows with the light of belief that all the ugly and good-looking incidents have a purpose and meaning, all being the servants of God. Even, belief gives such a power to the person that this person can see, understand, and digest the meanings of things beyond time, past, and future.

On the other hand, disbelief can have different types: persistent disbelief, purposeful negligence-oriented disbelief, lack of knowledge, and ability-oriented disbelief.

Persistent denial or disbelief can be a result of the person's personal invested interests (fame, money, etc) who knows that there is a Creator. They know that God sent the Scriptures and the prophets. But due to mostly identity, position, fame, or wealth-related concerns, a person may not accept the message although he or she knows that it is the truth from God.

The person makes an intention and inclination to acquire an action. The seed of acquirement is inclination and intention. The concept of free will is the intrinsic quality of free choice in belief. If we can review the two schools of belief: Strong and free-willed belief and already present belief- there is a fine line between them, and both are similar. Below, the diagram shows the process of free will (acquirement) leading to one's free will within the notions of inclinations in oneself.

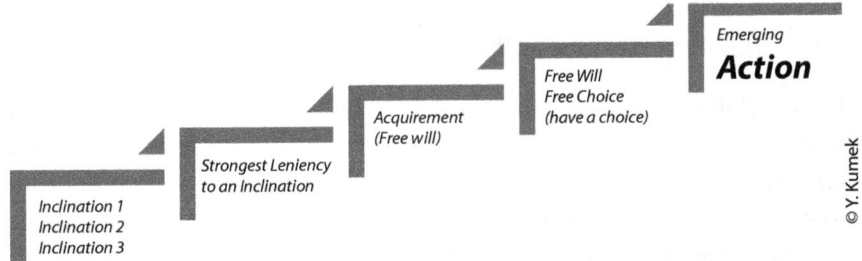

The Process of Inclinations in Oneself Leading to Free Choice and an Emerging Action from the Person

According to the above diagram, the creation of the action by God emerges from the inclination of the person. One can also replace certain words in their non-technical usage in the common language. In this case, the word intention of the person can best fit to the stage of acquirement or free will according to the above diagram. Sometimes, one can or cannot identify one's different inclinations for an issue. Then, after the dominant inclination with strongest leniency, one then takes a purposeful, calculated, and deliberate step with intention. Thus, the word intention in popular usage can equate with the word acquirement (free will) in the above diagram. Therefore, the word 'free will' is used as a technical word in the fine discourses of belief. On the other hand, the word 'intention' is used more as a non-technical term but with its general popular usage in all other fields of religious sciences such as in the sayings of prophets or religious laws.

In another perspective, a person in the short span of a lifetime can incline to his or her disposition and attach to it. It becomes most of the time difficult for humans to change their dispositions. This could be like the law of inertia in physics, a force acting against the notion of change. In a positive sense, the specializations in one field can add a value to one's attachment in one disposition. Therefore, if the person does not engage in regular self-reflection to diagnose constantly where his or her inclinations are with their purpose, then an entire life can be spent in an initial disposition that the person has encountered. The Scripture verses constantly engage the reader with this.

People do not want to change their given or initial dispositions where they initially find themselves in.

Difficulties and Problems of the Method of Comparison in Knowing God

In the methodology of comparison in the human realm, one should know that the person is a creation with endless limitations. Therefore, one cannot use the human realm to fully compare and contrast in order to know God. In this perspective, a human's realm can be only an image but not a real tool of comparison with God, the Infinitely Powerful, All-Knowing, Ever Existing and Everlasting, The Eternal, The Mighty, The All-Wise.

In another perspective, all the funny problems come into existence if one does not realize the difficulties and problems of the method of comparison for knowing God. One cannot compare Necessary Being, the One Whose existence is Absolute, Always Present, and Not Dependent with anything or anyone with a creation whose existence is limited and dependent.

In this sense, different formation of creeds within different religions have been representative and stemming from these problematic, unrealized complications and difficulties of comparison in understanding.

Here are some examples: the case of referring to God as father to mean caring, protective, or implementing just authority; the case of referring to God as having a son to give a value or to elevate a human's status because he was special and therefore God sent the son to earth to guide people; the case of thinking God to have an attribute of tiredness so that now God needs to rest on a day; the case that God does not create the bad, ugly, or evil so that there should be Satan responsible or any other gods responsible for this; the case of imagining God with anger, and to be an authoritative, androcentric or patriarchal being.

These are all problems stemming mainly from human limited understanding of constructions, or thinking due to comparison analogy when not knowing who God is. There are billions following these notions without going to the essence with a simple methodology: God is the Creator. All others are created as Aristotle concludes in his journey of logical deduction [5].

The true and genuine understanding of God follows with the primary guidelines of the Scriptures and the sayings of the prophets. Then, reason and experience follow.

One should know where to stop the comparison. In other words, one should be always aware of the limits of comparison and the limits of thinking. Stopping with etiquette, morals, and respect while knowing the limitation of oneself with humbleness are the main tools. Therefore, some religious people can also be trapped in temptations, paranoia, and wrong wanderings of mind due to not knowing this etiquette, morality and the methodology of limits with humbleness and true humility.

The Infinite Divine Will Power of God encompasses both the cause and result. In other words, sometimes people make mistakes by imagining the Divine Will Power of God, (referred to as willpower or intention) as something linear. In other words, in a case of a premise that 'if this happens, then this happens…' or 'if this does not happen, then this does not happen…'. So, if there is no apparent reason or cause to humans, we cannot fully say that the result would not be this. In other words, if a person gets sick by eating food, we cannot say that if he did not eat the food, he would not get sick. But from the perspective of fate and destiny, one can say, "We don't know." On the other hand, the group of people who believe we are controlled by predestination can say, "It doesn't matter, the person would still be sick," giving no credence to the cause, free will, or free choice. Conversely, a sect among the religions may say, "No, the person would not be sick," giving full authority to the cause, to the reason. In other words, making free choice will not be dependent on the intervention of God or willpower.

Another mistake in this approximation of comparison, for example, a person can make a small simple block toy car from wood. Then also, hundreds of people can come together to build a car with complex systems of self-navigation with fuel options of gas or a hybrid electric system. For any person observing these two cases, the latter will be more difficult to build and accomplish then the first simple toy wood car. But, for God, there is no notion of difficulty.

One should remember within understanding of free will, its acquirement and application, the Real Effective Cause of our free will is God. In other words, God creates the outcome of what the person wants with his choice of inclination, acquirement, intention and action. The laws in nature can assure structure and order to ensure the free will, choice, and execution of this in the world of causality. For example, the case of fire not burning Abraham is an example of a reminder to humans that the Real Effective Cause is God. In other words, the existing structure and order in nature through scientific laws are created by God. Therefore, God can order a scientific law not to work as in the case of fire with Abraham.

One should remember that the value of a human is according to his or her essence. One's essence is according to one's effort and struggle. The worth of one's effort and struggle have value according to the value of significance of one's intention, purpose, and goal. One can see this in the below diagram to make it easy to understand.

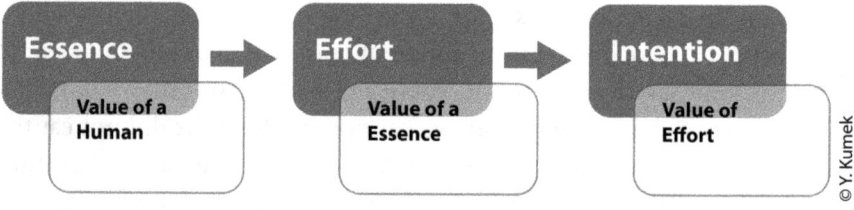

MEETING AFTER YEARS

There was a lamp which did not work for years. Mackenzie was hopeful that one day the lamp would work and give its light as in the old days. One day, Mackenzie was reading the scriptures and thinking about the meanings and possible interpretations. At that time, she really needed more light to focus. She touched the switch of the lamp and the lamp gave its light. Mackenzie started laughing, "You know when to work!"

IN PRACTICE

Everything is controlled by God. The living and non-living things can be a misleading classification in religious terms, as even the non living have a spiritual life. The so-called non-living things such as rocks or stones also glorify God according to the scriptures. Some people even witness their chants. In the above story, perhaps, the lamp did not want to miss the opportunity of giving and sharing its light while Mackenzie was engaged with the Noble Book of God, the Scriptures.

Value of Human in Religion

One should remember the learning process of a person in all of the above discussions. A person's learning skills mainly are built up on the methodology of comparing and contrasting towards increasing one's knowledge. In other words, a person looks around the objects, beings, incidents, and experiences and deduces causalities and results. This is the area where inclinations form. Then, the person intends to execute the inclinations with one's free choice and free will.

On the other hand, God is not like humans. The person makes a mistake to fully deduce meanings about the Creator by using the same methodology of analogy and comparison. This is a major mistake of humans in executing the free will and free choice. In other words, the methodology of comparison and contrast cannot be fully executed with the unseen. It cannot be fully executed to have the true knowledge of God. Therefore, there is a guidance needed. In this perspective, the scriptures from God, the Scriptures and the sayings of the prophets serve as the key to implement the notion of a 'guided method of comparison and analogy'. In other words, the person can acquire the true knowledge of God with the same method of comparison and analogy with the guidance of the Scriptures, the sayings of the prophets and by understanding and normalizing the limits of comparison for the unseen and especially for God. The discussion here mainly underlines rationalizing the limits of the execution of free will and free choice.

In this perspective, a person not aware of this, cannot rationalize fully the notion that the One, God, knows all of the inner dynamically changing feelings of a person in the heart, continuously showering thoughts in the mind, forming inclinations, and actions in secret and in public.

The case is that due to their free will, acquirement, and choice, they will not change their position of belief due to their stubbornness. God knows that they will die in that state.

One should remember that God creates everything, and God is the Real Cause. Humans and Other Spirits are given free will and free choice. Due to their free will, acquirement, inclination, and struggle of their usage of free will and free choice, God creates the action of what they want.

One should also remember that the Divine Mercy, Caring, and Graciousness is much more beyond than the Divine Justice and Accountability.

Therefore, a lot of times a person may be asking constantly for an evil outcome (knowingly or unknowingly) with his or her free will but God can be delaying the outcome of what the person is asking due to the Infinite Divine Mercy and Graciousness. If it is justice, the person should immediately face the constant insistence of his or her evil renderings. In other words, God is treating the creation with utmost Mercy and Graciousness. If God treated creation with what they deserved they would be in a severe deserved situation. This merciful treatment of God for humans alone necessitates praise and recognition for God.

God gives structure and order to everything. God controls, interferes, and creates constantly with complete perfection. This can be in the macro scale for humans such as galaxies, stars, and the universe, or in the micro scale relative to humans such as bacteria, viruses, and other beings. In this perspective, a human with consciousness, mind, and natural innocence knows that most of the things a person does not have any say or control over anything they choose to do, or what their body does internally or externally. Even, within oneself, the person does not have any control over his or her heartbeats, the processes occurring in the digestive system after eating food, the communications in the parts of the cells, etc. So, this is fully and perfectly in control of God with the Full Divine Power. Then, God gave a tiny portion of control called free choice or free will. Accordingly, God creates the results of this person's choice. For example, the person can choose what to eat. The person can choose how to spend one's time. But at this small scale, the person is responsible for his or her choice.

The second category consists of the people of purposeful negligence-oriented disbelief. These people can know the essence of belief, but they can be more in the state of 'I don't care. I want to live my life as I am living now'. These people may change. The attitude of indifference and not having concern for the purpose and meaning of life may not engage these people until they are hit by an evil-seeming incident in their life: deadly sicknesses such as cancer, near-death syndromes, or losing an attached value, for example: a job, husband, wife, or kids.

The third category is disbelief by the lack of knowledge. This person may not truly know what is right and wrong from the true sciences of religion. He or she may know sometimes but may not have the ability to change his or her condition because of weakness, laziness, or addictions. When lack of knowledge is combined with personal spiritual weakness and laziness, this person can be stuck in this lifestyle for a long time. These people may have a lot of guidance from God when they increase the true knowledge about God and about the true religion. With his or her new life of true knowledge with the scriptures, and the genuine teachings of the prophets, the person can be uplifted by God from his or her weaknesses and establish a new lifestyle with new positive people on the true path.

Disbelief is an attitude in thought, verbal discourse, and action. Belief is an attitude in thought, verbal discourse, and action. Disbelief is knowing, but not appreciating. Belief is knowing and appreciating. Disbelief is arrogance. Belief is humbleness. Therefore, if a person humiliates or makes a joke about something related with the building blocks of belief and the respected items ordered by God, then this person can have the attitude of disbelief and then be led to disbelief. Even in the thought process, if there is this attitude, this may again lead the person to disbelief. Here, a person who does not know or wants to genuinely learn is in a different category. Therefore, scholars historically try to establish the methodology of closeness to God. Closeness to God can be simply defined as 'to remove from mind and heart what is <u>not</u> about God'. It is because the human mind constructs the relationship with God with deficiencies therefore the negative constructions or these deficiencies should be constantly removed. It is these false and deficient constructions of humans due to their normal human limitations, but God is Perfect with all Divine Attributes and Names.

Belief is accepting and believing all of the structures and details of the true faith, creed, or belief. The concept of selective belief or acceptance of the teachings of the scriptures and the prophets is presented as disbelief.

Belief and disbelief are opposites of each other. Therefore, if one exists, then the other cannot exist. There is no mixed state or classification of belief and disbelief. A person can have the qualities of belief or disbelief, but one belongs to one group or the other. A person can have belief, but when he or she lies, then this person has the qualities of disbelief. A person can have disbelief, but when this person is ethical and honest, then this person has the qualities of belief. This notion is a fundamental concept of difference between the minor-extreme and normative-majority stance of religious understanding. The minority-extreme stance was that even with grave oppressions or sins, a person may have no belief; versus the normative stance in which a person can have belief, but by violating religious law, the person is considered to be a sinner.

Belief is a perspective and the state of heart and mind. Although the legal schools and the ways to act require belief to be verbally pronounced, the real state and essence of belief are in the heart and mind. Therefore, there were a lot of ancestors, the prior practicing pious religious people, who were using this positive uncertainty to increase their relationship with God until they die. They were genuinely fearful of meeting with God, uncertain of whether they had genuine belief or not in their hearts, even though they dedicated all of their lives in worship and good action. Belief is an attitude, psychology, and perspective of the person.

Belief is an attitude. The guidance from God comes with attitude. In other words, one can also say that guidance from God comes as a result of this attitude. In that perspective, one can look at classical belief books of religion such as Taftazani, and see that he mentions guidance from God is a light, due to this attitude of internal and external critical thinking with experience and open-mindedness [4] with different signs of God in nature or in one's consciousness. In another perspective, one can explain this guidance from God in the field of mysticism as the experiential attitude of open-mindedness, ethical behavior, humbleness, and struggle to practice [6]. The guidance in all cases is from God. Guidance leading to belief is a state of merging this sincere attitude of struggle with the true and correct knowledge about God and religion. This is the main guidance. After this stage, there can be different levels of guidance through practice, and keeping, upholding, and refreshing this initial state of belief.

Belief is also the asset of the person. Any possible danger that can challenge the health of belief should be addressed immediately. If not, it can spread in one's spiritual heart and metastasize in the person's true and genuine relationship with God.

One of the possible dangers in this relationship is sin. If the effects of the sins are removed with repentance, then the relationship with God can grow potentially and positively. Another challenge to uphold a sound belief is unnecessary and useless engagements. Another one is less praying and remembrance of God.

In all cases, one should realize that belief is the biggest lifetime asset of the person, if the person does not give value to it and endangers it with unnecessary and purposeless engagements, then the person can lose it.

Psychological Example of Disbelief and Belief

A person is granted life as a privilege from non-existence to the world of fears and unknowns. As this person is expecting mercy, in actuality sicknesses, accidents, fears, anxieties, and evils like an enemy attack this person in everyday life. When the person looks into nature and reasons, this person does not find mercy, but darkness. When the person looks at outer space, stars, planets, and meteors, the possibility of them crashing into earth makes the person tremble and even more scared. Finally, the person finds that the only solution is to reflect more in silence and to meditate. Then, his or her conscience becomes as if it would explode.

In addition, this person looks at his or her needs, and abilities, strength, and power, and understands that he or she is weak, poor, and very limited. This person knows that no one can truly help them even though they ask for help. She or he starts seeing everything as an enemy on the earth and as an alien. She or he regrets living and curses being in the world.

On the other hand, when the person enters onto a straight path, when the person's heart, mind, and soul are illuminated with belief, then the previous disbelief-related psychological perspective becomes colorful, delightful, and filled with light.

When the enemies attack this person, such as sickness, accidents, or other evils, this person asks for help and protection from God, the All-Powerful. When the person thinks with all her or his internal faculties and emotions, they all desire eternity and not dying. Knowing that there is an eternal life after death, then this anxiety cools down and the person becomes calm with longing for God and the afterlife and not scared or fearful as before.

When the person looks at outer space, the stars, the moon, and meteors, now he or she understands that they all work together under the control of God. The person sees them all as friends and signs from God instead of seeing them as something scary and intimidating as it was before.

Wherever or whatever this person looks at now, everything tells this person, "Please don't be scared and fearful from us. We are all servants of God."

When the person compares these two states and perspectives of disbelief and belief, this person truly appreciates belief, religion, and God.

THE REALITIES, OUR WEAKNESSES, AND OUR SHORT LIFE

One day, Kayla got some bad news about her work. Later that same day, she heard that her mother was put in the hospital having suffered a possible stroke. Then, she got sick. She said to herself, "We are so weak, and our life is short. There is no one to take refuge in except God."

IN PRACTICE

Turning to God in both ease and difficulty is the key. Sometimes our weak willpower stops us from turning to God in our down moments. Yet, there is no real solution all the time, whether being in need or not, other than to turn to God.

Belief and Excellence

Belief and excellence, or disbelief- they are all attributes of the heart. In this perspective, humans do not have the skills and authority to truly know and judge if someone has belief, excellence, or disbelief even after the person dies and meets with God. This is the action and position of the heart. There are signs of belief, excellence, disbelief, and telling people you are religious but not being religious. The religious laws are based on external affairs but not the internal affairs in these fields of belief.

True Belief and Spreading Religion

Belief necessitates a fear for the displeasure of God, a fear of not appreciating the favors of God, and accordingly, a fear for the consequences of an accountability, all the time, including when there is no one around.

The reality of belief and one's relationship with God reveals its true disposition when one is alone. If someone wants to spend time in solitude to pray, worship God, and makes this one's top priority in life, and take the most pleasure in being with God when the person is alone, then a person can show the signs of being a true believer.

Why is telling people about God and about religion important? First, every person is created in a state of pure natural innocence. Therefore, sometimes, this natural disposition is referred to as a true believer. In the original state of creation, everyone is in a pure, clean, and natural disposition of religion which can be called innocence. It is interesting to note that a person can feel the traces of this innocence in the early morning hours when a person immediately wakes up. One can call this perhaps a 'pseudo true believer' or innocence state. At this time of the day, the person is not exposed to all of the artificial exposure of the thoughts and feelings acquired over the course of the day. Therefore, if one really can look at oneself at those times, the natural innocence can be gripped and saved against the evil encounters of the person's self-thoughts and depression states during the day.

Secondly, the prophets and signs come into one's life to justify the witnesses that God has sent evidence into one's life. Therefore, there is no counter logical argument of the person with his or her free choice in front of God in the afterlife. In this perspective, the Prophets in his lifetime can ask his followers this question: "Will you witness me in the afterlife that I gave the message to you?" So, this shows that the prophets also have accountability of fulfilling their mission and they will also be asked about this responsibility on the Day of Accountability.

A possible reason can be that it is mainly people's attitude that they do not have fear and respect and appreciation of God, the Most Merciful, the Most Caring.

The spreading religion perspective in order to establish caution is for the results of an evil. In a simpler way, it is a warning for them against evil outcomes because it is at least expected to stop an oppressor by telling them the consequences of their evil and scaring them into being fearful of the accountability. If this person still has some soundness of mind, then he or she may say, "I don't want to continue this evil because I don't want to be in prison" for example.

Order, Chaos, and Meanings

The word falsehood can signify that in this world, in the universe, and in the creation, everything has a meaning and purpose. Nothing is random. There is no chaos. There is no pessimism. This word is repeated in many places in the Scriptures to allude to this effect. At a personal level, it is expected that the person needs to get a meaning from everything in his or her life and that everything comes with a meaning, message, and purpose from God. Therefore, as the person gets closer to God, this self-awareness becomes more sensitive, sharp, profound, and perceptive within oneself. In other words, all of the externalities of this person become internal. All of the externalities are internalized through the interpretation of their correct meanings.

This perspective can take the person to a level of thinking, reflecting, interpreting, analyzing, deducing meanings, and applying. From this standpoint, one can now analyze this and similar verses to allude to these notions.

Prioritization

Although as humans we need each other, we need our family members, friends, and social engagements, there is the notion of priorities in one's life. In this perspective, there will be times the person will be left alone due to either isolation as a result of disputes or arguments or self-isolation due to not getting preferred attention from others. These are the times that can hit the person hard if he or she does not have priorities in one's life. Either the person can fall in deeper depressive states by blaming others and increase this isolation. Or the person can use this time to focus on the priorities that are preferred by God.

Well, one can ask the question, why this should come at those times but not other times? Because the person is distracted and heedless although he or she may claim the opposite. In other words, when the routine is broken with unexpected cases that the person depends on, then this case is referred to as evil in our contemporary language. Yet, these are the times that can be opportunities to boost one's relationship with God. Especially, if the person humbly and logically performs self-reflection. Self-reflection can always keep the balance of priorities in one's life.

Lastly, we always have the desire to belong somewhere. Yet, this identity is embodied through the notion of the above discussion of one's life priorities to coincide with the ones that are preferred by God. These people with these identities will have the real happiness in this world.

OUT OF TROUBLE MAN AND MARRIAGE IN HEAVEN

There was a poor wise fool that Henry used to know. Each time Henry met this man he said, "Thank God, I am out of trouble." He used to call him "out of trouble man." One day, Henry attended a funeral. He saw the out of trouble man at the funeral and gave him a ride after the funeral. While they were chatting in the car, Henry asked him, "Are you married?" He said, "No, I am not now, but I will be in Heaven. I am looking forward to it." Henry said, "What a level!"

IN PRACTICE

It is suggested to get married. There are always exceptions to general rules. There are people who may not be married due to dedicating one's life to learning, praying, and teaching. They may feel that if they get married, they may not fulfill the rights of a spouse. As in the above story, there are a lot of wise ones who may have a high spiritual level with God, and they may disguise their identity by acting foolish sometimes. They are called wise fools. The wise fool in the above story did not get married in his life and perhaps dedicated his life to worship and solitude with an intention of getting married after death in Heaven.

Deity, Humans, and the Religion

Existence and Non-Existence

The creation of everything has alike and equal position for God unlike humans' engagement of value systems which range from difficult to easy. A creation can be more complex and bigger in structure than the other.

Yet, their level of creation in terms of equality is the same for God. We use the term equality to avoid terms such as easy or difficult, bigger or smaller, etc. These are all valid terms in the human realm of the constructed systems of values. The absolute actuality of this is the Transcendent Reality.

One can consider here the example of a scale. If we consider two heavy objects of the same weight and place one object on one side of the scale and place the other object on the other side of the scale, then they will be equal, in balance and equilibrium. Similarly, if we consider two very light objects of the same weight, and put one of them on one side of the scale and put the other object on the other side of the scale, then they will also be equal, in balance and in equilibrium as well. If we imagine the same massive star on each side of the scale, then there will still be equal regardless of their size or massiveness balancing each other. If we imagine the same lightweight fly on each side of the scale, then there will still be equality regardless of their minute size balancing each other.

Yet, if there is a tiny difference on one side of the scale, then that part of the scale will win over the other side.

Similarly, in our human renderings and approximations, one can possibly understand the notion of existence and non-existence to be similar to this equal plane on the scales of possibility. Whenever and if God wills the order, God brings that thing into existence. In this regard, this thing can be a massive star or a light fly, it does not matter. God knows best.

The Purpose of the Scriptures Related to Present Christianity, Islam, Judaism, Buddhism, and Hinduism

If one reviews the major world religions, one can realize that the Scriptures with the teachings and practices of the prophets aim to restore the original and authentic teachings about Divinity through the pillars of true monotheism, oneness of God, for the original and authentic path of God.
One of the diversions of religion and altered scriptural theologies from the true, authentic, and original teachings of the scriptures and prophets is due to applying a human valuation system to the Transcendent Reality of God.

One of the main reasons and purposes that the Scriptures were sent with the prophets was to restore the belief, creed-related teachings of these altered scriptures and prophetic teachings into their original forms as sent and revealed by God.

There are many examples of this problem of human constructed value systems being applied to the Realm of the Transcendent Reality, God.

One can realize that the Scriptures constantly address this problem of the human construction of value systems with the Realm of the Transcendent Reality, God. All of the time and especially in these cases, one should really maintain one's humbleness, humility, and etiquette and morals with God as humans are all in need, weak, and all dependent upon God.

Localized and Boost Treatment

The learning process for a person to develop new skills is primarily built upon a person's methodological approach of gathering information, arriving at conclusions based off this information, and reaching logical comparisons and contractions that lead them toward increasing their knowledge about the subject. In other words, a person observes their surroundings and experiences and deduces casualties and results. At this point, dispositions form and the person makes the choice with their free will to execute an action based off of new inclinations.

Again, God is not like humans. The person can make the mistake of fully deducing meanings about God by using the same methodology of analogy and comparison about aspects of the creation. As discussed previously, this is simply impossible. Therefore, there is a guidance needed. In this perspective, the scriptures from God, the Scriptures and the sayings of the prophets serve as the key to implement the notion of 'guided method of comparison and analogy'. In other words, the person can acquire the true knowledge of God with the same method of comparison and analogy with the guidance of the Scriptures and the sayings of the prophets and by understanding and normalizing the limits of comparison for the unseen and especially for God. The discussion here mainly underlines rationalizing of the limits of execution of free will and free choice. It also indicates the necessity of knowledge directly given by God about the guidelines of knowing our Creator through the Scriptures.

If one can realize how these problems are addressed and treated, then we can hit the root disease of this cancerous tumor to treat even a metastasis of the entire body of the creed system. The approaches of the Scriptures' treatment of cancer and the modern medical treatment of cancer are different. The Scriptures' treatment replaces the cancerous cells -in a way similar to the very precise gamma knife treatment- with healthy and benign cells appropriate to that tissue. The modern medical treatment only kills these cells without much replacement. Yet, the body that God has created is expected to replace these death cells with the benign cells.

In the physical body of cancer, the doer is God by regenerating the benign cells. In the spiritual cancerous disease of the heart and mind, the doer is God with the treatment of the Scriptures and the prophets. All of the teachings of the prophets are revelation from God. The sayings of the prophets and the actions of the prophets are unrecited revelation unlike the required disposition of the Scriptures as the recited revelation.

Irreconcilable Representations	Clarification
Multiplicity, trinity, duality	PURE MONOTHEISM, One and Unique Creator, God.
Absent/passive God	Constantly Intervening, Full Active, Full Alive, Infinite God.
Human qualities for God such as sleeping, unawareness	Always in Full Control, Always in Full Awareness, God.
Randomness, chaos, without ownership	Full Ownership, Control, Structure, Order as set by God.
Proximity and piety related partnership with God	No Partnership in Authority and Decision Making. Only and except by the ones that God gives permission or enablement.
Absence of Knowledge of God with time boundaries and other boundaries	Full Control of Knowledge without any time boundaries and without any blockage of concepts such as internal or external, or obvious or secret.
Absolute and True Knowledge can be acquired only by mind. Therefore, mind or intellect is above the revelation/revelation.	True and Absolute Knowledge given only by God. A religious community can have more true and absolute knowledge given by God as compared to an educated philosopher as a miracle similar to the case of the prophets. True knowledge necessitates mind and humbleness/humility with the enablement, Graciousness of God.
This universe, earth, and galaxies are only the ones. We discovered everything. Therefore, we are powerful.	This universe, earth, space, and galaxies that one knows with his or her limited knowledge are nothing compared to the Dominion of God, Therefore, one should be humble.

Deity, Humans, and the Religion

God became tired and rested.	God is far beyond human concepts of social constructs such as being tired due to difficulty. Human valuation and constructs are NOT valid in the Realm of Transcendent Reality.
Applying human value systems to the Realm of Transcendent Reality	God is far beyond and always higher than human constructions of any type of human valuation systems, so be humble and submit yourself to God on the path of the Scriptures with the actions of the prophets.

A similar above analysis can be made to hit the root disease of a cancer carried by many.

Irreconcilable Representations	Clarification
Illusional monotheism: such as trinity, multiplicity as reflected in deities as represented with different attributes of the same reality, or not explicitly naming God, the One but using metaphors such as nature, the one, etc.	God is One and Unique. Have the true oneness of God. Do not mix illusions with realities.
Causes as the real doers. Therefore, being dependent on the causes, multiplicities, rather than being only dependent on God.	God is the only Independent Being. Everything is dependent on God.
Applying human value system to God such as birth, parenthood, spouse, etc.	God is Unique and far beyond the values and necessities of creation.
Applying human value systems to the Realm of Transcendent Reality	God is One and Unique. There is no other being similar to God.

One can find other, similar, or different diseases addressed in the Scriptures with more treatment sessions.

THE HEALTH OF FAITH & PRACTICE

One day, Edward was reflecting on the difficulty of keeping one's submission, faith, and practice healthy as the person gets promoted in life in different worldly engagements. He said to himself, "Although you are trying, at any time your submission can become diseased. It is very disgusting to get these diseases constantly and one needs to put in effort in order to constantly clean it."

IN PRACTICE

Yes, it is very difficult to maintain the healthy state of submission, faith, and practice. It is not impossible with the grace and enablement of God. Yet, if one can detect the feelings of disgust as a symptom of these spiritual diseases, then that is a good sign. The person has the alertness and self-awareness of the incoming diseases. The next step should be to make an effort to clean them with asking forgiveness and engaging oneself with practice.

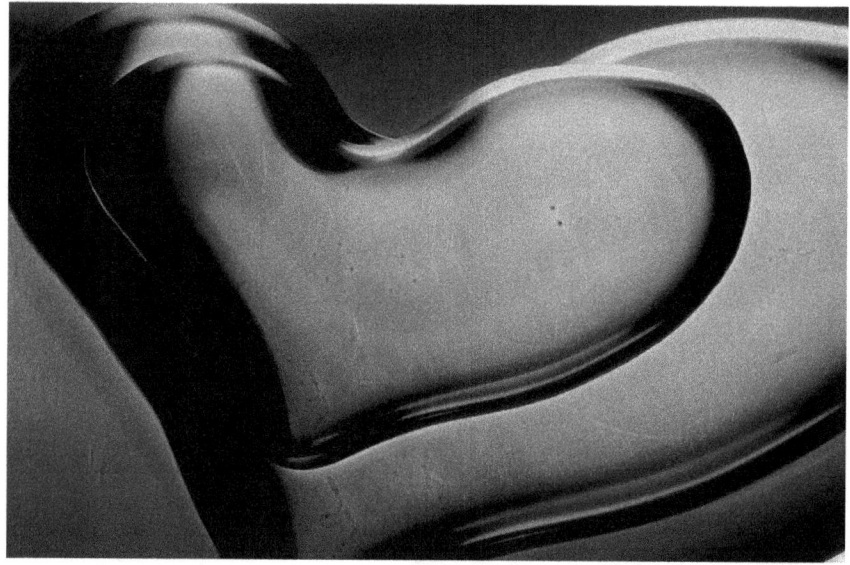

© Pixabay

Human Language, Reductionism, and the Role of the Scholars

One should remember that the Scriptures use the human world's realities of language to address the problems and offer their solutions. If the Scriptures were non-understandable and just highly theoretical, there would have been a disconnect from humans. The comprehension and accessibility would be difficult and only for few. Therefore, as people specialize in each field including the science of religion, the technical words have a perfect meaning for the experts who are few.

Yet, the majority may not understand what religion's reality and essence is. In this situation, the experts have the responsibility of explaining these ideas in the reductive language for the general population. This duty is very critical and should even be maintained at the times of dire need.

Prophets served this vert purpose. The prophets have the highest level of belief and know the attributes of God. The prophet said, "If you knew what I knew, you would laugh less and cry more," [7]. In this regard, the position of the prophets, scholars, and teachers have the responsibility of always reducing and adapting what they understand from breezes of the Divine knowledge and experience to the comprehension level of the humans.

One should remember that in the causality of humans, humans are attracted to the content if they have any relevance, understanding, and connection with it. Therefore, adapting the language for humans in the content of the Scriptures, in the sayings of the prophets, and in the practices of the prophets is present with a purposeful wisdom. Most people do not understand the scientific language of technicalities. They understand teachings in their popular language of culture and time.

In other words, everyone and everything speaks in its own language of habitat. Humans talk and understand within the social construct system of language in their habitat. The Scriptures primarily address humans and therefore the Scriptures use a language that humans would understand.

Birds view the world according to their understanding. They understand Divinity, Oneness of God in their own language. Imagine a critical food item for the birds. By using its valuation system of importance for their sustenance, the hoopoe bird can give an example from an item that is so critical for the species of birds. Then, the bird very well and precisely can explain the true Oneness of God. The story of a bird, hoopoe, in this context understanding Divinity with a food item is mentioned in the Scripture.

For humans, anger can show displeasure of someone with sadness and regret about something.

Being angry possibly with sadness and regret, can lead to some undesired outcomes for humans. Also, humans can have anger with regret.

God mentions and encourages the believers not to act with the state of anger but to forgive people.

For God, anger can mean the displeasure of God for an evil act but not a deficient quality as in humans. God does not have human qualities of regret or sadness. God has the displeasure of humans' renderings of evil, sins, and oppression, yet God is All-Wise, and executes the Divine Will with Wisdom and Patience.

Peaceful States of Heart

When we consider the essence of our pure soul and purpose in life, one should remember that the soul referred as the spiritual heart desires the peaceful spiritual states. The words peace or submission can indicate this reality.

The peaceful state of the heart is achieved by attaching the heart with only, but only, God [8].

In this regard, the state or level of excellence or perfection is complementary with the peaceful state of heart.

In other words, the peaceful state and level of the heart is achieved only by attaching the heart, but only, to God. This is only accomplished with the state and level of perfection.

One should remember that we get encouraged and proud with our world titles of president, doctor, PhD, MD, chairperson, etc. Yet, these titles are all pseudo and fake and temporary and are only valid in the realms of this world as these titles are generated by humans in their value system.

The titles such as 'peaceful heart' are given by God to people who after lifelong struggle against the internal frictions of themselves and against the struggles by Satan. This struggle may be in a society where the person is all alone challenging the norms and values all by himself or herself without any recognition or valuation. There can even be a case of humiliation and mockery by others in that society.

Therefore, the title of 'peaceful heart' displays itself afterwards by attaching the heart only to God.

This is a level available for the people of God, for the true and real people of God. Not all of the companions of God can reach to this level. Yet, all have the possibility and potential to have a peaceful heart at different levels.

When we further analyze the peaceful state of the heart as achieved by attaching the heart to only, but only, God and leading to the level of 'peaceful heart', one can further elaborate on a person not asking his or her needs to be met from anyone except God. One can now consider the position of Abraham, when he was challenged as a sole person in his society. He did not ask anyone's help except God.

One can again realize the level of a peaceful heart that comes with the peaceful state as achieved by attaching the heart to only God. Therefore, one should realize the key repeated terms to achieve this level.

SILENCE, SMILE & PEACE

Ariel wanted to be always in peace and tranquility from God. She used to constantly smile and keep silence. If she needed to talk, she used to say it in a few words in a very nice and gentle voice and tone. Then, she used to stop talking and observe silence and smiling as it was most of her engagement. She used to always experience peace and tranquility as granted by God.

IN PRACTICE

Talking, harshness, and ungentle behavior in sound and voice can destroy one's spiritual honey of belief. The taste of this honey is tranquility, peace, and calmness as granted by God. The prophets were the embodiment of this trait. They used to smile much and talk less. When they spoke, they used to utter few words with very deep and wisdom-embedded meanings. One of our problems today is that we do not how to stop talking once we start it.

Social Constructs and Religion

Normalizing the Human Reality

The Desire of Being What You are Not: Adam and Satan as Angels

It is interesting to note that there is something appealing about being an angel. Satan was another spirit but wanted to be like angels. Adam was a human being but wanted possibly to be like an angel.

In both of the above cases, one can see that either angels have very appealing features or there is another reason that we do not know.

Yet, the test and trial are to be pleased with what and how God created this being. In other words, if God created a being as a human, Other Spirits, man, woman, black or white, the person should be pleased with God's choice as a form or dress of creation. This shows an attitude of acceptance, humbleness, humility, and submission to God. This is a notion not as an identity tag but as the essential trait of all creation. In this perspective, all of the creation has the noble title of worshipper of God. However, when a creation is not pleased in which dress, form, or species that God has created it, then this is a sign of an implicit or explicit ingratitude to God. Therefore, praise as a gratitude and thankfulness to God is the essence of belief [9]. Heedlessness, denial, and the desire to be who or what you are not is the essence of disbelief.

Yet, God still gives the person what they ask for. For example, Satan was permitted to be with angels. Yet, when everyone in the gathering received the order to respect the new creation of God, Adam, Satan could not handle maintaining this company of angels. Angels submitted to God and yet, Satan showed a trait that was hidden in him for a long time. It could have been better for Satan to be humble and accept who he was and stay with his other fellow beings if he was not going to disobey God when he received the same order as the angels. Or, it could have been best to still keep the company of angels but ask for forgiveness after his disobedient position.

On the other hand, when Satan tricked Adam with a similar tool to instill in Adam to be like angels, then, when Adam realized his mistake, he immediately asked for forgiveness and still maintained his position with God.

Why do people want to be something or someone other than their own selves? Why do people not accept what is given or granted to them in the cases of things that they cannot control such as how they are created as humans- man or woman, black or white, in China or in America or in Africa? Why do people not accept themselves to be humble and human? Why do people then not accept other humans' or their species' advice? This person who is giving advice can be a friend, parent, teacher, messenger, or prophet of God.

All of these above discourses and discussions can be possibly due to the arrogance of the person not realizing his or her real self. The demagogies can extend with similar discourses and beyond. Before all of the futile claims, demagogies, and spiritual wanderings, the key for the person is to realize who he or she really is. This realization will happen eventually. But, if it happens with death, then it will be too late.

CAT HANGING AROUND WITH HUMANS

There was a cat who used to hang around with humans. She did not like to hang around other cats because she found them very annoying. This cat always saw humans as perfect and wished that she was a human like them. When a person entered the house, she used to come next to them and hug them. Camelia understood this situation and told the cat, "It is not as you think."

IN PRACTICE

One of the sicknesses of the heart is that we do not like to be who we are, but we want to be like others. God gave us so much. Thanking and appreciating increases the bounty. In the Scriptures, it is mentioned that if the person thanks and is appreciative for all of the bounties, then God will increase them more. In the above story, Camelia felt that her cat was in the same position. She tried to tell her that the humans are not all perfect with their evils and their diseases of the heart.

© Pixabay

Normalizing the Mistakes

When the person is prohibited from doing something, human nature has a tendency to incline towards it. It is natural or normal to fall into sin, error, or something harmful even though one can instruct and warn a person or a child of the harmful outcomes of this engagement. As mentioned by the prophets and scriptures, there is the normalization of this concept that it is normal to make mistakes, sins, or errors but the best one is the one who accepts one's mistake and turns to God with repentance and humbleness as exemplified by Adam. So, this approach can be important in both adult and child education- the emphasis of teaching the notion of normalizing mistakes. However, the most important thing is to ask forgiveness from God and to connect again and again. The teaching of what to do if one makes a mistake in childhood and adult education is paramount.

For Satan, it was not easy to accept Adam. Satan was swearing and Adam did not know a possible being or creation who would be swearing and yet at the same time possibly lying. Possibly, Adam could have forgotten the command of God that he should not have approached that tree, as the name of the human is 'the one who forgets'. The approach to learn and to teach in the relationship with God is resetting one's position with the Creator, God, and asking forgiveness. One can see possibly that Adam may have wanted to worship like angels and forgot the prohibition of God about that tree.

GOING BACK AND BACK

One day, Jim did something that was considered a sin or a displeasure of God. He promised before to himself that he would not do it, but he did it again. He was ashamed of himself in front of God. God gave him so much. He said to himself, "How would I face God?" He went to pray. Then, he started crying and asked forgiveness and said, "Oh God! Where can I go? There is no one who can forgive my bad and ungrateful treatment towards You. Please forgive me. You are the

Most Forgiving. You like forgiving. You are the Most Merciful and the Most Compassionate."

IN PRACTICE

It is important to constantly go back again and again to God until one dies. There is no one who can help a person in reality except God. If God wants and accepts, then the means follow. If God does not want to accept, although others seem to comfort the person, there is in reality no one who could help this person. In the above story, Jim embodied a prayer suggested by the prophets, "Oh My Sustainer and Nourisher, I oppressed myself many times with sins, rebelling against You. No one can forgive those sins except You. Please forgive me with a forgiveness from You. Have pity on me. Indeed, and certainly, You are the Most Forgiving, Accepter of Repentance and the Most Merciful and the Most Gracious." [34][1]

Manifestations and Reflections of Names and Attributes of God

Human problems in the true oneness of God. The manifestation of will, power, and knowledge of God is Infinite. Humans may get some type of clue about the different Names and Attributes of God through the Manifested Divine Actions of God. These are all manifestations or reflections. They cannot be replaced with the Real. Yet, one should remember that the manifestation of these actions of God can give a person true knowledge about God.

Yet, one should realize the manifestation of different Names and Attributes of God constantly, in similar and different places, contexts, and beings. Looking at only one Attribute and Name of God in only one manifestation and trying to approximate one's understanding about God through only one Name and Attribute cannot be the best way to approach the true knowledge of God. One can love one Name and Attribute of God a lot. Especially, one can realize the manifestation of one Name and Attribute of God in particular in the spiritual travel of a person. At this state (level), the spiritual traveler can be overwhelmed with this One Name and Attribute of God. When this state is over, then the traveler comes to the reality of knowing and realizing other Names and Attributes of God.

This shows that one can approximate to true knowledge about God by studying and experiencing different Names and Attributes of God. The effort of a wholistic and comprehensive approach in understanding different Names and Attributes of God is extremely important. This can lead to true oneness of God and no doubt in the belief of a person. Therefore, the prophets encourage us to know and to memorize the 99 Names of God in the tradition. There are more Names of God than the 99 Names. The Names of God are infinite as mentioned in different texts. Yet, the compilation of 99 Names as a collective unit is a famous tradition encouraged by the prophets and mentioned in the sayings of the prophets. This can be the initial stage and training for religious people to struggle constantly for the true knowledge of God leading to true belief with no doubt.

Similarly, humans may get some type of clue about different Names and Attributes of God through the Manifested Words of God. In this regard, the Scriptures are all Words of God sent to humans. These Divine Words indicate and explain to us different Names and Attributes of God. One should remember that the manifestation of these Words can give a person some understanding about true knowledge about God. These are all manifestations or reflections in our realm. They cannot replace the Real.

One can realize the manifestation of different Names and Attributes of God constantly, in similar and different places, contexts, and descriptions as mentioned in the Scriptures. Looking at only one chapter or verse through only one manifestation and trying to approximate one's understanding about God through only one Name and Attribute cannot be the best way to approach to the real and true knowledge.

One can love one chapter or verse a lot. This is normal and virtuous. The effort of a wholistic and comprehensive approach to understanding the entire body of Scripture is extremely important. This can lead to true oneness of God and no doubt in belief in a person. Therefore, the prophets encourage us to know and memorize certain chapters and verses. This can be the initial stage and training for people to struggle constantly for the true knowledge of God leading to true belief with no doubt by approaching the Scriptures fully and wholly.

One should remember that all of these Words are manifestations or reflections. They cannot replace the Real. These are all manifestations or reflections in different realms.

Yet, one should differentiate all of these manifestations and reflections in different realms from the Real Attributes of God.

Embodiment of Supplication

One should remember that everything in their real realm of Dominion known by God is noble. In their interaction on the plane of Faith, they have the external skin of evil, good, or neutral. The causes in the realm of Faith are covers to protect one's belief so that they do not lose etiquette and morals with God in terms of attributing blame and evil to God.

The Nobility and Highness of God requires the causalities to act as a cover in the executions in this world hiding the realities behind them. The Oneness of God indicates control and surrounding of everything beyond the causalities. God is the Real Cause behind all apparent causes.

God is higher than all of the human value systems. One must admit this reality and always negate the problematic issues and replace them further.

One should remember that a person on the true path of religion has the assigned privilege of the use of the term God. This can be translated as 'my Sustainer'. The pronoun 'my' shows a level of acceptance. Therefore, it is similar to a person who is already accepted in the house. He or she is not an outsider but is now an insider. Now, the person moves forward learning about increasing his or her rank in this house.

Human Value Systems as Social Constructs

The Scriptures are perfect, flawless, and complete. The discussions of skepticism and doubt are all human related concepts or social constructs.

There is a human framework of judging and valuing things. In this regard, discussions related to insects, worms, or flies can be lowly in the human realm of valuation system.

Yet, to point out this flaw in the human social construction of the world, systems, and values, God gives examples in the Scriptures to challenge this error in human thought process. In this case, some humans have an implied assumption that if someone talks about topics considered lowly by humans, then this undertaking may not fit the nobility of the person.

In this regard, this could have been the case especially in the pre-modern societies and eras. Today, with the advancement of science, we are all amazed with the structure, order, and system in both micro and macro worlds. For an intelligent person, these examples go beyond discussions of social class implying caste systems of external nobility which lack the needed disposition of focusing internally on the essence or the content rather than assigning values according to the externalities. All of the caste systems and nobility-related renderings can somehow have relation with the internal spiritual disease of arrogance.

One should remember that we give relative values to the beings around us. One refers to this as social construction. In other words, one can claim that we use a language that we construct ourselves. This relative language is our own construction system of values through our experiences.

God created everything. Everything is a creation of God. The sun is a creation of God. A fly is a creation of God. An atom, an electron, a proton, a neutron, and a quark are all creations of God. They are all under the command and order of God. They are all servants of God.

The notion of good, evil, ugly, or beautiful are all means, definitions, and values that we view in our world among the creation as another creation. All of the creation is a servant of God. All of the creation has the absolute reality of being a servant of God.

All of the creation has the same expected purpose of remembering this submission while fulfilling its assigned responsibility on the earth. All of the creation recognizes and fulfills its assigned submission except some humans and Other Spirits. God has given the potential to humans and Other Spirits to exceed all of the creation in their submission with their effort and Graciousness of God.

Conversely, they can be at the lowest of the low of all creation in their worship with their choices. The epitome of all creation who surpassed all of the creation in worship is the prophets. The lowest of the low of all creation that is at the bottom in the worship is Satan.

Golden Rules to Remember

One should remember that humans form their value systems according to their own understandings.

In their reality and essence, everything has a high and valuable purpose and meaning. Although some of the things in their externality may look ugly or evil, yet in their essence, they have beauty and purpose in their utmost relationship purpose of being existent among the creation.

In this regard, God is the God for all of creation regardless of their reference point to the humans.

Sometimes, due to the style of the speech and writing, the examples from different valuations can amplify the effects of the message.

Sometimes, describing unpleasantness, a secret, or evil has a purpose of explaining the problem, disease, and case fully. Yet, one can realize the etiquette and morals of these explanations in the Scriptures in that it allows the reader to receive the message without the side effects of doubts or unpleasant imaginings. In other words, the etiquette and morals require one to describe the evil or unpleasantry with modesty and balance.

It is important to use popular speech, dialogue, terminology, and language when making a call to others. Disconnect in the language can cause misunderstandings, alienation, and isolation from the message.

Claims of Self or Nature-Related Existence

If a person takes the smallest observable or measurable particle, let us say it is an atom. Each atom has a different number of electrons, protons, and neutrons. The identity of each element is determined by the number of different atoms. Each element formed by a different number of atoms can have different qualities.

Social Constructs and Religion

It is statistically impossible for the electrons, protons, or neutrons forming each atom to come together and form an element by themselves. This element will form with different combinations into DNA, RNA, protein, or an organism. Then, this organism will have life. Then, within all the micro- and macro-systems, there will be a structure or balance. This is illogical, absurd, irrational, unfounded, inconsistent, and impossible.

If we assume the above at micro or angstrom levels (10^{-6} to 10^{-9}), then one can jump up to the macroscopic levels where the units of measurement are at the speed level of light (10^8). In all of these systems, regardless of their size, there is a perfect structure, order, running systems, maintenance, rules, and guidelines.

As a simple example, one can witness in our social life, if there is a small unit or a corner store, people assign duties to prevent chaos. As the organization become more complex as a corporation, then the rules, with a hierarchy, structure, and order can become more detailed in order to run this corporation to minimize the problems.

Similarly, how can a person assume no hierarchy, or no authority in the universe, with perfect, fine, and detailed running of super complex systems both at microscopic and macroscopic levels? This is illogical, absurd, irrational, unfounded, inconsistent, and impossible.

On another note, one can witness the reality of wars, destruction, and chaos in human history, when there is the case of at least two or more people running for authority and leadership. They fight each other to get this authority.

Our human minds sometimes hide behind impossible possibilities far from logic in order to not face realities. The extrapolation of the discourses of evolution is another avenue that people in the scientific communities hide behind with wrong assumptions and interpretations in some scientific discoveries. In other words, God can create different species in different forms. Their shapes, heights, and looks can change. God mentions that the Divine has created living things from the water. All have a context. Interpretations and extrapolations of a possible truth with generalized and statistically impossible renderings are not deemed to be scientific.

On another note, meaning, value, and goal in our short life require structure, order, and nobility. Purposelessness, meaninglessness, or having no value invites chaos, destruction, pessimism, and lowliness. Connecting everything in the universe with the randomness of statistically impossible outcomes is accusing them of lowliness, purposelessness and meaninglessness. Yet, everything in the universe except some humans know their position in the universe.

For example, A person enters a house which has beautiful and detailed artistic and technological motifs, appliances, and features. While looking for the owner of this house, this person sees a smart TV, a smart refrigerator, and an oven in the kitchen. This person looks at the colorful marble stone with its natural designs on the kitchen countertops. Then, she looks at the natural oak wood flooring. The flooring color and its touch instills in her a full array of different feelings. This person wants to touch the natural wood with her bare foot. Then, she realizes that there are different types of lighting with different artistic designs of light fixtures. When this person turns on certain light fixtures, they give yellow light. The yellow light reflected on all of the designs and the artistic rendering of the kitchen makes the person take different pleasures from this beautiful combination of complex and artistic designs with a gushing of emotions in her heart. When this person turns off the yellow light and turns on the white light, this person now sees everything differently with different emotional renderings and perplexities. In all of these mystifications and puzzlements, she develops a very high admiration for the house owner. Then, she says to herself, "The house owner has the ability to establish this structure and order. This house owner should have very high skills of beauty, artistic, and intelligent design."

Another person enters the same house and he is amazed with everything similar to the previous person. Yet, this person gets stuck in this amazement and would not be able to move on to the next step. Then, he idolizes these items in the name of science as laws generating these appliances, smart TV, fridge, and light fixtures.

In the above analogy, the first person is the person of belief. She is not stuck on the beautiful and complex systems which necessitate structure and order. She moves on to the next step of finding the Establisher of all of this perfect design and system. The second person is the lost wanderer sometimes referred to by the term 'depraved'. Since this person does not have a clear perspective, meaning, and goal, he or she may get stuck on immediate incidents and not see the realities beyond them. When a person does not have a meaning or goal in life, in reality that person does not even know his or her own self. They can be also called a person who is a 'lost wanderer' in our popular language.

WORLDLY & SPIRITUAL-SEEMING ACHIEVEMENTS & FATALITIES

One day, Isabel was engaged in reviewing her life incidents. She was trying to play and re-play the incidents in her mind. There were cases of worldly and spiritual-seeming achievements. She said to herself, "From the movie of my life, it looks like I have had some fatal spiritual crashes in both arenas. In the cases when I lost the real goal, the ends got stuck in the false means."

IN PRACTICE

Anything or everything can be a test or trial. Alertness with humble and full refuge in God is the key for safety measures.

The Obsession with Impossible Statistical Arguments

One can ask: Why are some people obsessed with getting behind arguments that are statistically impossible?

When humans do not want to take the step of belief with their free will even though everything may be clear, simple, and straightforward in front of them, they choose to find something that will calm their denial. Yes, it is up to the person to decide with free will to believe and say, "I believe in God and other pillars." Or, the person can run behind the impossible possibilities to try to calm his or her inner screaming that ultimately tells this person, "Go back to God."

Yet, at the end there is no compulsion in religion as mentioned in the Scriptures. With all the clear verses, signs, and indications, the person needs to make a choice using free will. The whole secret of free will, responsibility, and trust is to *make a choice*. God mentions in the Scriptures that if God wanted it to be so, everyone would believe in God. Yet, the expected goal for humans is that they themselves will make this choice with their intention, free will, and will clearly verbalize their stance. One can review the explicit verbalizations of individuals in the Scriptures to indicate their stance.

At another level, some people possibly do not methodologically follow the epistemology of logic. They follow one step after another. They use the premises and propositions of logic and philosophy. They start off using some evidence correctly. Then, in between, or at the end of their statements or arguments, they end up either arriving at a wrong conclusion within the epistemology of following these steps, or they insert unwarranted assumptions in order to fill the gaps in the argument and conclude the narrative. An example of this can be found in the popularized clashes between the scientific communities/defenders of evolution theory and the Western religious authorities.

Within the context of religion, the Scriptures, and the acts of prophets, one can find the verses about the creation from water. Then, there is a change. In the context of evolution theory, the doer of the action is always hidden or named 'nature'. Some of the teachings of this theory are compatible with the teachings in the Scriptures and actions of the prophets. One can reconcile these two perspectives and then clearly present the conclusions with a choice of either 'a simple logic, accessible and straightforward', Initial Cause, God; or, very complicated, statistical impossibilities of using some other language such as 'nature, laws, universe, etc.' in order to minimize the religious terms.

One of the underlying logical problems occurs when a person assumes something that is unlikely and statistically impossible will happen without any proof. Then, the person runs behind the doubts, impossible possibilities, and self-depressive states of uncertainty with darkness of anxiety, fear, chaos, stress, and insecurity. Yet, the person of belief can start the journey by taking the initial step of religion. Then, as he or she goes further, the certainty is expected to increase. This can be referred to as positive states of certainty leading the person to confidence, happiness, peace, and calmness in this world and in the next. The emerging cases of skepticism, agnostic approaches, and others can be some examples. Critical thinking is important with fine, positive, and constructive approaches. Skeptical approaches leading to negative, depressive states of uncertainty can be self-destructive to all unanswered questions.

Another level of problem occurring in the popular culture is happening in these clashes between the scientific communities/defenders of evolution theory and Western religious authorities. There are people who have somehow already alienated themselves with their religion. Then, they go full-heartedly and sometimes blindly behind these popularized and scientifically stamped discourses in the replacement of their religion. Then, it becomes backwards if the person does not agree with some of the up-trending popular stances promoted by some scientific communities of journals, articles, and associations.

In this case, mostly, the people who follow these popular up-trends can be the general public who somehow identify themselves as 'modern', 'cool', 'open-minded', or 'educated'. Yet, their knowledge about the essence of these clashes can lack scholarly depth. They may have more peripheral knowledge. At that level, they can view something impossible as possible without methodological thinking and critical analysis. In these cases, 'to follow' the up-trending cool norms and normalize this peripheral knowledge in themselves can become natural. This type can be observed more in the states of heedlessness due to the lack of awareness of the reality of these clashes and conflicts.

One of the key points of the above arguments is related with the intention and purpose of engagement of any knowledge. If one genuinely tries to search as a matter of life or death or with a vital purpose, then the person will not risk or even entertain the impossible statistical arguments relating to one's afterlife, purpose, meaning, and goal in life. They will believe in God and search and increase their knowledge for oneness of God through the teachings of the Scriptures and actions of the prophets. On the other hand, if a person views this question as a matter of regular commodity without giving much importance to it, especially within the genuine search of purpose, meaning, and goal in this life and in the afterlife, then they will follow what others say. They will be on the periphery of this search dragged by the popular and cool trending approaches of their time and society.

At another level, in the cases of scholarly stance, the person can see the clear distinction of the impossible. Yet, they may not make the simple, logical, straightforward, and accessible choice of belief but rather make the choice of being in doubt with statistical impossibilities. In these cases, either the preventing factors can be related to some spiritual diseases of group identity or self-identity due to arrogance, jealousy, fear, and others. Or, if they die without making a clear choice while searching the positive states of meaning, purpose, and goal in life, they may be in the borderland between heaven and hell as mentioned in the Scriptures.

In the case of public stance of following the popular culture, they are not aware of their real state. They do not fully know why they follow.

Or, in some cases, like Aristotle [5], they use the mind and premises of the logic with very delicate accuracy and conclude with an approximation of true dedication of all acts to God. Yet, since there is no reported Divine Guidance (revelation) similar to the Scriptures and Actions of the prophets, they may not practically include the language and understandings related with oneness of God and reliance on God.

In religious epistemology, knowing human limitation is a virtue and required condition in the approximated knowledge related with the Transcendent Infinite Reality—God. In other words, knowing and understanding something fully, especially with mind, can mean surrounding that being intellectually. Yet, limited knowledge cannot surround the Unlimited. Humans should know their limits of etiquette and morals in their knowledge and relations with God, the Unlimited. The true knowledge and experience with human limitations can only be approximated with the guidelines of the Scriptures, actions of the prophets, mind, and experience.

Sometimes, a person can be investigating or researching the truth or a phenomenon. In their research, they may find a pseudo, side product. Then, with different constructions or approaches, they may try to justify this pseudo-effect or side product as the reality or truth of this phenomenon.

This case is very common in the experimentations of natural sciences such as physics. When a physicist is acquiring data from a sample, it may be difficult to understand and then interpret what could be considered as 'noise'- unwanted, pseudo-effects as compared to the real goal of this experiment. Many times the data is correct, but the interpretation of the data is misleading. Other times, the analysis is correct, but the conclusion is false.

In the personal journeys of relation with God, there is the case of humans who cannot truly attach themselves to Oneness of God, the Unique, the One, the Creator, due to this multiplicity of background noises with varieties. A good scientist or physicist can differentiate these noises from a genuine signal or sign with different wavelengths and frequencies. Similarly, God gives every human the abilities and skills of mind and experience. With a genuine thirst of searching for the results or answers similar to performing scientific research, God guides the person to find the real signal- the Scriptures and the prophets- as long as the person maintains humbleness with the motivation and struggle to find and research about it. In this regard, gaining knowledge and learning is also one of the critical elements in order to understand what is genuine and what are pseudo-noises as compared to genuine and authentic signs.

A particle or an atom has a billion different possibilities of doing something. It becomes part of an element, system, human, animal, planet, space, or galaxy. Then, this atom becomes part of the application of a scientific law. The existence of this scientific law in the universe depends now on the critical motion, effect, or contribution of this particle in this system. Among billions of possibilities, the adventure of this tiny atom in its motion, choice, existence, and role... How can it take this role? Then, one can think of billions of atoms with these roles and different purposes being assigned to different tasks. How can they be assigned? After this assignment, in this complexity of billions and more, how can this system be maintained?

The answer is easy and straightforward. This answer is accessible to all levels of learners. The answer is not only for the elite intellectuals in universities with artificially generated titles of recognition in these communities. It is not like the case of impossible statistical arguments that one uses to soothe or trick oneself with, and it is not like the impossibilities of popular terms of skepticism or others.

God is the One who creates this atom and all others. God is the One Who orders them to form a structure. God is the One Who maintains this structure. God is the One Who establishes the rules as scientific laws as the laws of God. God is the One Who can give at any time the order to these atoms or elements to act in the way that God orders them contrary to their present duties. Fire not burning Abraham is one example [10] of these atoms or elements not acting according to the natural laws but a clear sign that they work under the command of God however they are ordered to do so. All other miracles are other examples.

When an atom works under the command of God individually, it still works under the command of God when this atom becomes part of a system, galaxy, human body, plant, or an animal. This atom does not work for or take orders from the scientific laws or natural laws. Natural or scientific laws are our abstraction and the language of our social constructs to identify these principles in the universe as created and maintained by God.

The Word 'Nature' as a Social Construct

Let us view the word 'nature' and how it was popularized and constructed, especially in the last two centuries. This was a replacement of the language for God, especially in the Western world, as one of the reactions of the alienation from the religion. Then, as a socially constructed phenomena, the word nature has been used in scientific journals to connect people with an entity which was not clearly defined.

When they were asked, "Do you mean 'God'?" Then, the immediate or defensive response can be, "No, we believe in science." Then, when asked, "What do you mean by nature?" They may reply, "All of the scientific laws." Then, if the conversation follows as, "Why do you give a hierarchy as a collective body of laws called nature?" They may reply, "Because there is a governing body." They may be asked, "Then, can you refer to this governing being as God?" Then, they would insist and say, "No, we want to call it nature."

When I was teaching at Harvard Divinity school, there was a student. She mentioned that she had a discussion with another person who identified herself as an 'atheist'. At the end of their ongoing conversations, her friend agreed to use or pray to a term called 'mother universe [11]. These can all be social or personal language related constructs. Yet, one really needs to go back, find, and detect the alienating reasons in the language referrals and reconstruct them with the closeness of God.

One can note that, the term used in the Scriptures, 'laws of God', and in some of the scholarly writings, the term of 'servant of God' can refer to the laws discovered in different natural and social sciences today. In other words, God can establish all of the structure and order through different means such as what we refer to as scientific laws or theories, or nature as popularized today.

Sometimes, our social constructs due to political, cultural, and other reasons can replace a word and people may not realize what they really mean when they use it. It can be a reaction, as mentioned, to the religion in this case.

God has infinite beautiful and perfect names. In religion, as long as one can find God with one beautiful name, that is still accepted as long as they understand that the Creator, God is One and Unique. It is expected that the person can increase their knowledge without any implicit and explicit partnership with God in their connection.

In this regard, a human lifespan can have these cases of multiplicity due to one's lack of knowledge of one's own self in detailing one's own knowledge. The case of using a socially constructed word such as 'nature' is one of these examples. Yet, as the person learns more through mind, heart, and experience related education, then it is expected that that person can embody that there is unity and there here is only One God.

At a very clear stance, God mentions these humans' false social constructs by addressing in the Scriptures with a very simple but straightforward question, "Is there a book or scripture from 'nature', 'scientific laws', or other social constructs telling you to follow them or what you follow?"

If nature, social, cultural, political, or any identity constructs you have, have sent you a proof or a book, just bring them and let us see.

This is a very straightforward and simple challenge and the answer is, "No, there is no deity who makes this claim except that God clearly, strongly, and in a very straightforward way mentions that God is the Creator, God and the Scriptures and the prophets have been sent by God."

In other words, God sends a book and scripture. This Book, the Scriptures, clearly and strongly states without any social construct that this is from the Creator of all universes so that we can place our social constructs in a framework. Yet, people follow things as shirk that have no clear sign or indication.

If we have a mirror that we hold towards the objects, it will reflect an image of the object. The object in the mirror is formed due to properties of amalgam derived from a mixture of mercury on a glass surface [12]. Yet, we cannot say that mercury, or amalgam, or glass creates the image. God gives these properties to these elements.

On the other hand, if we do not move the mirror towards different objects, there is a mirror, but it is not functional. It is just staying there and waiting to be explored. Yet, a person comes and takes an action on it by holding it towards the objects. Then, then there is an image. In these perspectives, these natural laws or chemical properties do not have mind, intelligence, willpower, and a goal to do something. They are all the creation of God waiting to be explored as different signs of God [13]. The person can ascertain a meaning and use critical thinking for their own purpose, meaning, and goal in life in order to increase their belief and attachment with God with certainty.

At another scale, if a person watches the stars in the sky on a summer night, there is a sense of amazement, astonishment, awe, wonder, and admiration. To express these inner feelings of joy or admiration, a person who knows and certainly believes in God may say, "Wow! What a perfect creation that God created, this marvelous, beautiful, perfect structure and order! Thank you, God! You give me the ability to recognize, and feel joy and pleasure from all this wonderful, fabulous, and remarkable system structure! Thank You, thank You, thank You!"

On the other hand, the person who may tend to identify himself or herself as an atheist or with similar or more popular identifiers in the same scenario of watching the stars on a clear summer night, may say, "Wow! Look at the stars! It is such a nice, amazing, beautiful, perfect structure and order! Look at the scientific laws of physics! It is so amazing! Thank you, science!"

In the above case, the person gets amazed by the perfect structure and order. He or she assumes or animates 'science' in order to express his or her gratitude and thankfulness. The laws themselves are concepts labeled as 'science' in our social constructs.

In a more popular culture, people in the above categories may say, "It is so amazing! Thank you, nature!" Or, "Thank you, mother nature!" Or, "Thank you, universe nature!" (in more intellectual circles).

Let us analyze the above cases and try to identify the similarities and differences.

In all cases, when a person finds a perfect structure and order, first they get amazed and astonished. This amazement gives them joy, pleasure, and admiration. This overwhelming admiration and adoration rushes to one's mouth and tongue to verbalize them. Up to this point, everyone shares the same or similar points of amazement of inner boosting feelings regardless of if they are religious or not. One can remember this notion in the separation of state and church. In other words, people may call the inner experience up to this point 'secular'.

Then, in this verbalization, everyone tries to locate where to give credit, respect, admiration, adoration-to something or someone.

The ones who are alienated from religion tend to cover the reality with some alternative labels of science, scientific laws, nature, mother nature, etc. The ones who know the reality simply and directly utter the name of God, or the Creator from the deep parts of their hearts with full certainty, conviction, and full confidence. In addition, they embody this amazement, adoration, and admiration by supplication, and verbal prayers showing their constant amazement and adoration, gratitude, and appreciation to God. In this sense, this is called 'worship'. The word servant has the meaning of adoring and admiring something and following and submitting yourself. In this regard, it has this natural disposition of a person who has this amazement, admiration, gratitude, and love. Therefore, these moving, internal feelings of embodied adoration fuel up the person's body and tongue with remembrance of God many times a day through prayers, supplications, chants, and recitation of the Scriptures to appreciate and increase their amazement with joy, peace, and happiness in this world and in the afterlife.

On the other hand, the other ones who label themselves as 'atheist' or with similar labels have a hard time finding a good word and using it. They try to avoid saying God because they first identified themselves as 'atheists'. Therefore, they do not want to say something which would contradict their own selves and how they identify themselves. They try to update and use different expressions over their lifespans for years or generations unless they simply accept and face their own selves before they die.

Instead of doing this, it will be much easier on their souls, hearts, and minds to say God. Then, they can go back to the problems of why they were alienated from God due to their wrong constructions. Then, they can re-build their relationship with God with authentic, positive, and non-alienating realities with the Graciousness and Mercy of God.

Another example of this can be a small child observing a parade performed by a group of people. The people in this performance or parade walk exactly the same way, at the same time, and with the same hand, arm, and leg movements. A child observing the structure and order in this performance can assume an invisible rope is making everyone move at the same pace and in the same shapes forming an array of geometric structures. Yet, a very ordinary person knows that the people in the parade work under the command of a parade leader. They were first trained by the leader and the parade leader is still there to maintain the structure and order.

Similarly, God creates and trains the beings such as electrons, atoms, and other beings with the scientific training laws. Yet, God still maintains this structure.

In a similar sense, one can view nature as the art of God. This art is not lifeless or motionless like an art piece hanging on the wall. Yet, it has a perfect structure and order with life, service, and ecosystem. This art of nature is painted with the scientific or natural laws and is called laws of God.

Epistemology of Religion

Realms in Religion

Sometimes, some events can happen in one's life that can be a test, or a guidance from God. Other Spirits may have more interaction tools about matters concerning the unseen events about humans. They try to rationalize what is happening with the events if they are a test or not for humans.

Humans are most far away or at another level of interpreting the events depending on their connection with God. The level of connection with unseen realities in their real meaning can increase in the below order as:

1. Humans
2. Other Spirits
3. Angels

One can call this the world of humans and the world of the Other Spirits. The world of Other Spirits is in between the human world and the invisible realm as they may interact with both worlds negatively and positively. The case of Satan as an Other Spirit among angels, the case of stoning of the Other Spirits by angels, and the case of Other Spirits interacting with humans are all some examples.

TRIALS & TESTS

One day, Brody's best friends were playing pranks on him and taking his things. This time, they took one of Brody's best friends: his lamp. Brody was so upset and disturbed that he said to himself, "This is the third time! They are showing a childish attitude by removing my lamp again! I do not understand these people. They come to pray and look so pious, and yet, they do evil in the temple." Brody said, "I will leave it to God, and I am afraid the retribution may not be so pleasant."

IN PRACTICE

One should expect trials and tests although one should constantly pray to God for protection against them. Although a person may not do any harm to others, there will be people who will try to bother, harm, and sometimes abuse that person anyway. In these circumstances, opening yourself to God and then taking the necessary measures is important. Sometimes, it is important to be patient and not do anything. Sometimes, the person may need to take some measures with wisdom. Everything depends on the context.

DISCUSSION QUESTIONS

1. Discuss a time when you witnessed a conflict or situation work itself out better without your interference. This may be because you intentionally restrained your emotional reaction or it may be because of circumstances beyond your control, but the important thing is that, afterwards, you acknowledged to yourself that your interference would have complicated the issue.
2. Discuss a time when you accidentally made a situation worse by interfering, even with good intentions. What caused you to take action? Was it fear, anger, or another emotion? A desire to control the situation, or something else?
3. What is the value of exercising patience and wisdom in the appropriate context regarding improving one's relationships with other people?
4. What is the value of exercising patience and wisdom regarding improving one's personal relationship with God?

Personal Choices

This differentiates two groups of people: One group takes God as their main concern in their lifestyles. The other group takes and prefers a lifestyle other than God such as materialism. In this regard, although the value system of both groups may have a lot of similarities, in their essence, there will be a main and basic system in terms of their motivation or intention of the individual. Therefore, there would sometimes be clashes in understanding, communicating, and empathizing with each other. Even among the ones who have belief, there would be a spectrum of different people who may not embody the belief in the same way. Then, these criteria explain for the embodiment who should be a true protector for the person. There are a lot of religious people who cannot differentiate this basic premise between these two groups. In other words, even among religious people, one should be selective about whom to choose as a protector.

Religion and Western Philosophy

Natural and Social Sciences in the Scriptures

God established natural and social laws. This can be referred to as 'laws of God'. Today, we may popularly refer to natural and social laws as natural and social sciences.

One can find a lot of relations between natural and social laws or sciences as presented in the Scriptures as part of the laws of God.

Yet, in today's classification, natural sciences can include physics, biology, chemistry, and other fields. Social sciences can include anthropology, psychology, sociology, history, education, and some other fields. Humanities or liberal arts can include philosophy and sometimes religion, language, music, arts, and others.

In the Scriptures, one can find a lot of examples of transition from natural science-seeming incidents to the social science cases in order to increase relevance and meanings. In other words, Scriptures' approach to laws of God within disciplines is a very integrative perspective in deriving meanings and relevance.

From this perspective, different fields that are not as pronounced as they used to be, for example, social-physics, anthropological-chemistry, and other fields are already embedded in the content of the Scriptures and instruction. Yet until today, these perspectives of classification have not been popular until the recent increasing trends in interdisciplinary approaches in different sciences.

For example, Brownian motion is described in the field of physics as the erratic random movement of microscopic particles in a fluid, as a result of continuous bombardment from molecules of the surrounding medium. One can analyze this same observable and tested motion of these particles by transforming them to the fields of psychology, education, and sociology.

For example, if a child is constantly blamed by their siblings or parents similar to the continuous bombardment of the above particles, is there a display of erratic or random traits in a child? How is the personal identity of this child? At another level, if one analyzes the same approach for some groups such as ethnic or religious and others, if they are constantly blamed, broadcasted, or scapegoated for the evil, how is their display of their identities as a group?

When one analyzes the Scriptures, these transitions of natural sciences to social sciences and/or humanities is very vivid and there is no barrier. Yet, in today's classification of rigid separation of these fields, there seems to be a barrier that helps people to derive correct holistic approaches.

The Process of Perfection

One can observe the flow and tendency to maturation in the laws and sciences established by God.

These laws of God can be observed at different levels.

A seed in the soil can grow as written in the laws of God. Then, it can become a small tree, and then a big one. Then, it can give ripe and mature fruits. Then, over time, it can get old and die. The same process can be observed in the lifespan of a human. This similar process can be observed in the lifespans of animals, plants, and even in the lifespan of the earth. These same laws of God necessitate that the world, stars, galaxies, and the universe have an ending, as also mentioned in the Scriptures on the Day of Judgment is vividly described.

Both birth and death ceremonies are established rituals in all religions today as the major events. The Scriptures locate them in their authentic and real disposition as part of the laws of God in their importance of being either major or minor relative to the main purpose of the creation.

This main purpose is the recognition of these laws of God and relating to the real meaning of all creation with God through the lenses of belief. In this perspective, all the changes, major- or minor-seeming incidents can become irrelevant as long as the person has a relationship with belief with God Who is the Everlasting, The Independent, Who is Beyond and does not have these humanly cases of change, etc.

On the other hand, the person of disbelief is constantly in pain and fear of these changes in their own bodies, the changes outside in nature, and the changes in social structure through wealth, diseases, death, and other evil-seeming incidents.

One can visit the terminologies such as natural selection or survival of the fittest as presented and especially concretely popularized today. The word concrete is important to allude to the awkward approaches of dispositions of people not considering possible terminological problems. This especially becomes very prevalent when it comes to a point of defense mechanism of a group identity.

God establishes the laws. These laws can be referred to by people as science, theories, or scientific laws.

Individuals have lifespans, birth, growth, maturation, and then, wearing out in power, and death. Similarly, some of the species as a group in the past could have fulfilled their lifespan of existence and served their purpose at that time and space in the ecological system as created by God.

It is always the case of perspective, interpretation, view, and disposition of the person.

In this sense, the same phenomenon can be observed by two individuals, understood and analyzed, interpreted and narrated differently.

Both individuals can observe the change in species or in something.

One can say the "change or process is the process whereby organisms better adapted to their environment tend to survive and produce more offspring as the theory of evolution expounded by Charles Darwin [14]." Another person such as Karl Marx who lived at the same time as Darwin can also assert similar ideas affecting the others as possible trends of that era, along with industrialization, promoted the idea that power is the key essential for survival.

In this approach, the human being is viewed as a single entity who does not have any connection with his or her surroundings, but everything is based on power and interest-based relationships. Their success of survival depends on their own abilities of power, strength, and confidence as also indicated in the theory of survival of the fittest as "existence of organisms that are best adapted to their environment."

Yet, these approaches can bring in the society's selfishness, arrogance, disconnection from everything, and bring a huge burden of life on individuals trying to handle it by their own selves with their weakness. Yet, this person dies and kills himself or herself spiritually in life with fears, panic, and unknowns where the reasons can stop. A small invisible pandemic virus can instill so much fear in them with the fear of the unknowns and self-dependency on their own power but yet, leave them feeling helpless and weak.

The other person who is the person of belief views and analyzes the process of change, absence of some the species today, and their extinction as part of the laws of God.

He or she observes everything as part of the deductive reasoning of mind with experimentation, observation, and analysis as part of the laws of God. At the same time, he or she knows their limits as a weak creation in front of God and follows humbly the guidelines as presented in the Scriptures and actions of the prophets as part of the inductive reasoning.

One of the biggest evolving arguments of Western philosophy is around cosmology. Understanding of existence and the universe revolves today around evolution from water and the Big Bang. One can amazingly and miraculously again realize one more time besides many to witness the freshness of the Scriptures.

The Scriptures point to these two historical arguments, theories, and disciplines.

In this regard, a person of belief does not deny all of the possibilities of today's findings of science as part of the laws of God such as the living things in their relation with water and the Big Bang [15].

Yet, putting the framework of belief with the Scriptures becomes critical and a main pillar in their purpose and true understanding of cosmology with its reference to oneness of God.

Very interestingly, with the people of science, academia, and analytical scholars of different fields, we may not have much difference in what we say, and we agree on the deductive perspectives.

Yet, they may call these deductive reasoning 'sciences' and stop there.

Yet, we continue with more and know fully without any hesitation with certainty that this reality of the Big Bang and creation from water are just due to the simple fact of laws of God, the laws and science as established by God. We become more amazed with these affirmative findings, increase our knowledge and appreciate what is given to us by God in the Scriptures and the sayings of the prophets.

In that sense, the first category of people may imply intrinsic qualities of unappreciation, arrogance, confident-looking behaviors, recognition by humans or seeking worldly fame, wealth accumulation to gain power, and self-dependency leading to fear and stress but never being content.

The second category of people of belief entails appreciation for all of the blessings of God as part of their belief, humbleness, and humility in front of God and dependency on God. Therefore, this person is not fearful but happy, and consequently is powerful as he or she gets their power from the All-Powerful. They constantly recognize their dependency on God. They do not care about recognition from others seeking fame or reputation. They only do their actions to please God. They may earn wealth to help others in order to please God.

In that sense, a person of belief is more inclusive accepting science as well as the greater purpose behind it in this world and in the afterlife as instructed to us by God. This person fully knows that science is only simply a means but not the real cause. The Real Cause is God behind all the means. Yet, this person follows science to respect the laws of God, the laws and principles as set by God.

The other person just limits his or her perspective to science, unknowingly and implicitly expects from science in the social construction of the language and devastates himself or herself in this life with disappointments and devastates their life after death.

The same problematic approach of identities can be seen between the real religious people and Scriptures

One accepts all the books from God in their authentic form and recognizes different prophets at different times with a broader and wider true perspective. The other is confined to only one identity with exceptionally inclusive approaches of a group.

In this regard, the tag 'religion' goes beyond the identity but becomes a trait. This trait includes openness, open-mindedness, inclusiveness, logic, reasonability, balance, humbleness, humility, altruism, genuineness, kindness, spirituality, practice, health and hygiene, following the means and science, appreciation, gratitude, and expecting everything from God but not from anyone else. Therefore, when one reviews the term of religion, as it is used for different prophets, and other people beyond the group identity, it is used as a character trait and as the display of one's heart and mind.

The Content and Language of the Scriptures in all of It's Perfection

In these above discussions, one can realize another miracle of the Scriptures. The Scriptures are always appealing to the reader at different times with their existing understanding of science and nature.

One may ask: Why didn't the Scriptures explicitly mention the motion of the earth and circular shape of the earth? The answer is that people for almost a thousand years may have been isolated from the Scriptures

Epistemology of Religion

according to their understanding about it as truth. The Scriptures and teachings of the prophets are there to guide people.

Yet later when it was found that the earth was of a circular shape, then the Scriptures' verses were revisited and it was fully realized that the words used actually implied explicitly the circular shape and the motion.

Yet, we want to interpret according to our understanding of nature. Therefore, the style of Hidden—Safe is very critical to open these meanings. This style is part of the style of the language as rhetoric referred to as persuasiveness. In this style, although the meanings may seem obscure for a generation of people and time, this obscurity becomes clear for another group of people at another time in history with the advancement of science and changes of the civil and social norms. So, in its true sense, there are no unclear meanings, yet their meanings are waiting to be revealed, and opened by the right people at the right time in history. Therefore, continuous engagement with the Scriptures is critical with changing tools of time as it is very critical to discover these precious meanings as diamonds and pearls in order to shed light in personal and collective lives.

Most of the time, people give their judgments according to apparent, explicit, and literal meanings of the renderings. It is a good advancement that at our time in civilization, in education the notion of 'critical thinking' is emphasized to go beyond the literal or purely presented meanings of the data.

One can see again this breaking point with altered scriptures when the explicit language is inserted for the shape of the word as 'flat', and then when people discovered the opposite, there was a huge problem.

Yet, God clearly mentions this complementary, and fresh perspective of the Scriptures that there is no contradiction.

The Scriptures are always fresh, authentic, and real as the Scriptures are from God.

One should also remember that the revelation of the Scriptures does not primarily serve the purpose of the details of scientific discoveries. The meanings are there for everything. Yet, the primary meanings will be explicit such as oneness of God, afterlife, accountability, and the true purpose and meaning of everything in their reference to God. Then, the secondary meanings such as the details of scientific amazements will be embedded sometimes explicitly and sometimes implicitly.

'Why' for Religion and 'How' for Science

For example, if we analyze kinship relationships, why does a mother carry the feeling of caring for her child? Why do we feel bad when we see someone in pain? Why do lions or tigers as some of the wildest animals in depiction take care of their babies? Why do the birds take care of their babies? Why does a chicken sacrifice herself to protect her baby from a wolf or fox? Why does a perfect structure exist in a simple, microscopic solid crystal that leads to today's computer technology? Why is there a perfect structure in the orbits of the sun, the moon, and the earth with their perfect velocity that establishes equilibrium/balance with centripetal/centrifugal forces?

All of the above questions and many more are extrapolated from the Scriptures with the answer that all is by the Actions of God. The God as the Real Care-Taker or Care Giver, the Maintainer, and the Sustainer establishes the means through different vehicles whether people realize it or not.

On the other hand, science looks at the 'how' of the above questions instead of 'why'. For example, how does a mother carry the feeling of caring for her child? How do we feel bad when we see someone in pain? How do lions or tigers as some of the wildest animals in depiction take care of their babies? How do the birds take care of their babies? How does a chicken sacrifice herself to protect her baby from a wolf or fox? How does a perfect structure exist in a simple, microscopic solid crystal that leads to today's computer technology? How is there a perfect structure in the orbits of the sun, the moon, and the earth with their perfect velocity that establishes equilibrium/balance?

The answers to all of the above questions can be rationalized, interpreted, and explained with different natural and social sciences such as physics, biology, chemistry, psychology, sociology, and anthropology. Yet, these are all the means or laws, or theories established by God in order to show the Creations of God clearly, simply, and with accessibility for all levels of learners.

In the above perspectives, the questions of 'how' should lead to the questions of 'why'. In other words, the person should not be stuck on the means while trying to reach the ends.

In other words, the purpose, goal, and meaning are the questions that are given by the religion. In religion, one can also refer to this as *intention* as a formalized teaching. Execution of the actions to reach a purpose, goal, meaning, or intention comes as *secondary* to the questions of 'how' being answered as the scientific knowledge deals with them.

In this regard, the purpose, goal, and meanings are primary. Analyzing, understanding, and looking at the process can be secondary. That *does not mean* that the secondary or science is not important. It is as important as the initial step purpose, goal, and meaning. Once the person takes the initial step of intention, belief, purpose, goal, and meaning, then the latter steps of execution of this through science, actions, and means will support and substantiate this initial step.

Or, if there is a mismatch of intention and action, belief and hope, purpose and science, then these two will affect each other, either working in harmony of hopeful states of belief, or in chaos of depressive states of disbelief.

Purpose is the motivating factor for doing an action. In today's scientific educational terms, one can also call this "relevancy" [15].

Intention is the motivating factor for doing an action.

Belief is the motivating factor for having a 'hope.

Belief is the motivating factor for making the discoveries of science. This is done in order to increase one's belief and to fully attach oneself with certainty, certainty of knowing the names of God. In each scientific discovery and in theoretical sciences, one can witness and boost one's purpose and meaning in belief of certainty in God, in belief with certainty of the afterlife, and in belief with certainty of the other pillars. One of the qualities of a true believer is to have no doubts. In this case, certainty in the afterlife is not an option but a required case for a true believer.

Religion is the motivating factor for scientific inventions. Applied sciences such as engineering, medicine, business, and social sciences look for the relevancy to help humans and all of creation.

The institutions of endowment, advances in astronomy, physics, medicine, social sciences, and other disciplines in the golden ages of religion had this initial purpose, goal, and intention. Yet, a person or a researcher outside religion when analyzing this case, can merely focus on the scientific outcomes, and not the purpose or intention motivating these factors.

In this regard, increasing the belief through scientific discoveries and applying relevant technology to help humans and all of creation are within the fold of religion. For the ones who don't look or assume these engagements are within the fold of this true framework of Belief and Religion, they can use the scientific discoveries and applied sciences to discriminate, abuse, gain power, and make it exclusive and not inclusive for all of humanity.

Some people may not realize this order of theoretical sciences and applied sciences. Sometimes looking at the existing products in nature urges the person to analyze this structure and order and to go back to their initial intention and purpose in life.

For the people who are heedless, they may not care about the structure or order, but it may always be the case of selfish or interest-based relationships. In these cases, it can be important to show them the benefit of what they constantly receive in the exchange of something, so that they at least can go back to their intention, goal, and purpose and appreciate what they have. Although they may not initially care about what the big picture tells them about the purpose and meaningfulness of life, it can be important to remind them about how their interest-based perspective of life actually points and requires recognition of the Transcendent Reality.

In the descriptions of the verses of the Scriptures, God mentions different benefits of the perfection and balance of this structure and order with the recognition of Oneness of God. If one recognizes and accepts this reality, then this is called belief in God.

Yes, as we talk constantly and incessantly about this structure and order in the universe, one can ask: Why is this so important? Or why it is important for me? The answer is very clear, yet we sometimes assume it or overlook it without clearly stating and locating our own selves with the answer.

If one asks, "Why is the structure and order in the universe important for me?" Then, the answer is, "Because I benefit from all the structure and order. If there is no structure or order, everything is chaos. Everything is in destruction. There is no existence and there is no me. I do not exist. For me to exist, live, and maintain, I need a body, anatomical systems in my body such as a respiratory system, nervous system, circulatory system, excretion system, and others. I need an external environment or setting, residence, earth, and universe to place my body in so that I can exist and live. If there is no structure and order in my body, then my existence in a perfect environment or earth may not mean much because I need to first maintain my body. Conversely, if I have a perfect body, then chaos in my external setting such as earth may not mean much because I may not exist due to the chaos."

In simpler terms, the person needs perfect structure and order in order to exist and live. In other words, the person benefits fully from the perfection and structure in their own creation and in the universe. This is all from the Creations of God.

On another note, the name of the perfect structure and order that we witness can be called nature. The rules, principles, and scientific laws in nature can show us in detail this perfect structure and order. When there is a constitution in a country, it may be so inclusive, non-discriminatory, and establishing of security and peace, that we may be amazed with this perfect structure and order in these guidelines. Yet, they are all constructed and established principles by humans.

People who live in this country benefit from this security, peace, and safety as established by this constitution bringing structure and order in the society. They benefit from this 'privilege' regardless of realizing this benefit or not. People may even migrate to this country for this outcome and for the benefit of this safety, protection, peace, and security in this country due to its constitution bringing order and structure.

Similarly, in order to allude to the reality that humans constantly benefit from this structure and order, according to the interpretations of the meanings of the Merciful, this is the Name of God that indicates that regardless of being a believer or not, God gives sustenance, and gives them what He created in the universe with great benefits. In other words, regardless of their acknowledgment of the Giver, God still grants them benefit.

This teaching method can instill in the person the realization of this benefit that the person receives incessantly from the structure and order that God created. In other words, this verse constantly asks the person, "If you benefit from this structure, order, and blessings, then why do you deny?"

'Rabb' is used for God to emphasize the Creations of God. Yet, we do not realize this constant benefit we receive that is required for our existence and survival. We do not realize the benefit in this structure and order established by our God.

On a side note, one can find a possible relationship with the Name of God and Rabb, Creations of God. God as our Rabb and The Merciful allows everyone to benefit from this structure and order in this Earth.

On the other hand, the specific benefit of this and more from this structure and order in the afterlife can be observed only by the people of belief.

When one recognizes something as a blessing from God in this world, then they are called the people of belief.

In other words, this recognition, or appreciation can be called belief.

Yet, in this world, regardless of this recognition or appreciation or not, everyone receives and benefits from this perfect structure and order created by God. The people of disbelief in reality benefit from this structure and order due to the existence of people of belief being among them. When there are no people of belief left in this world, this benefit of structure and order is taken from them as The Day of Judgment occurs. The prophets mention that all of the people of belief will die before the destruction of this structure and order of the universe referred to as The Day of Judgment [7]. In other words, there is no purpose for the existence of this perfect structure and order for humans and Other Spirits if there is no one left in existence who recognizes and appreciates this structure and order as a blessing from God.

In the afterlife, the people of belief and disbelief are separated.

Now, there is a blessing with more structure, order, and beauty given only to the people of belief as they recognized before and they will continue to recognize.

One can see in the afterlife the continuation of recognition and appreciation for all the bounties of God manifested in this world and continuation of this manifestation in the afterlife.

In other words, when one constantly witnesses this interaction of purpose/intention and action, belief and hope, theoretical sciences and applied sciences, and belief and religion, then the person can be amazed at the level of harmony and perfection. In this amazement, or adoration of God, the person becomes the real servant of God. The word servant can linguistically be translated as 'someone who submits to another due to their deep love, adoration, and respect for that person'.

The embodiment of servant comes through worship. Prayers and others are expected to be the regularized and condensed forms of this verbal embodiment of being the honored servant of God. Prayers, supplication, fasting, doing good, and avoiding and stopping evil are all expected to be the regularized and condensed forms of these verbal and bodily embodiments.

In this regard, it is another blessing that God teaches us how to show adoration and worship to our Creator, God. As God is The Compassionate, The Benefactor, The Generous, and The Bestower, even in these acts of worship, God gives immediate benefits when we engage ourselves and more benefits and rewards after death. In reality, the immediate benefits and afterlife benefits do not need to be there because we are doing our worship to express our adoration, love, and respect that we are alive, existing, and constantly under the showers of benefits of structure and order in the universe as created by God.

Yet, if a person knows someone, you may not do anything for that person, but naturally as a human being you can just ask about, check on, and remember him or her. This minute act makes this person so happy that this person constantly sends gifts to this person. You know that you really did not do much, but this person appreciates it above and beyond. God is the source of all humanly appreciations. God has the Infinite Appreciation as the Real-Appreciator.

When a person shows this natural and expected step of remembering their Creator, God, then God gives huge benefits immediately, later, and in the afterlife. The person becomes someone living in Heaven both in this world and in the afterlife.

Now, after all of this, the person realizes these realities of how much it makes God pleased and happy by only recognizing and remembering God as One and Only. Then, the next step is remembering God in prayers and on other occasions as instructed by the Scriptures and the actions of the prophets, and comparing them with the huge, immediate benefits here, later, and in the afterlife.

When the person thinks about all of these and remembers how much God is pleased and becomes happy when being remembered, the person cries and cries, cries due to this deep adoration for God as being the servant, and has embarrassment of himself or herself due to not pleasing and making God happy as it ought to be, and cries not to be in heedlessness of selfish engagements.

Method of Religion

One should remember in any of the renderings of the Scriptures that one should primarily consider the initial and primary meanings through the methodology of interpretation. In this methodology, the understanding of narrations as explained by the prophets with their reason and early ancestors of the followers precedes the engagements of the diverse using other analysis in the contexts of intellect, time, and context.

With respect to our ancestors and the contemporary renderings of literature review, one can update the classical fundamentals due to the changing times and need. In this new updated methodology, the fundamentals in derivation of the knowledge and rulings.

1. The Scriptures
2. The sayings of the prophets

3. The data from natural and social sciences including culture and context
4. Analysis
5. Consensus' Consensus

Among our pious ancestors, consensus occurred with Guidance, the Graciousness and Mercy of God handling the same subject matter and coming out with a similar conclusion and forming the consensus by different scholars at different times in different regions of the world.

It may be sometimes questionable if each of the pious ancestors living at similar times in history or different times in history or generations did have access to the books written by these scholars. In other words, coming to the similar conclusions referred to as consensus at similar or different times of history possibly due to not having easy access to the full literature because of the limited tools of communication and publication, these scholars have arrived at similar conclusions with the Guidance, the Graciousness, and Mercy of God. This is another miracle of the Scriptures.

This is another proof of the authenticity of the Scriptures with the content and fundamentals as agreed upon by the ancestors. Independent experts at different times in history in different parts of the world reach the same conclusion without having much access to the prior works of the field as compared to today.

With today's easily accessible communication tools, one should review the data available in different disciplines with the experts of that field before going to the step of analysis. In this updated methodical approach, one should work together with the experts of the field when making analysis. Independent committees working on a subject can establish consensus about subject matter. Our accessible communication systems, emerging widely and quickly spreading problems in the matters of the religion can necessitate this consensus or consensus methodology during our current times instead of waiting for it to occur over time as has happened in the past. This approach will prevent more damages instigated by Satan and Satan's followers.

Including the data from natural and social sciences with the experts of the committees in that field before doing the analysis will fit in better as following the means as a way of showing respect to God as all the causalities, sciences, and means are created by God. One can refer to these means as social or natural sciences or 'servant of God' or 'laws of God' as mentioned in the Scriptures.

When we discuss the disconnection between the academic research and scholarship in practice today, this problem can be valid not only in religious sciences but in different fields as well. Today, secular publication curriculums dictated by the state departments promote relevance and embodiment of the academic knowledge in practice in order to experience the knowledge. In another perspective, there is an effort to minimize the disconnection between the theory and practice. Yet, the disconnect still exists. The students or seekers of knowledge can still be unmotivated due to this real and existing disconnect.

If we take one example, in academic articles in the fields of social sciences or natural sciences, there is a term, concept, or case that the article revolves around. The whole article tries to support this concept, case, or the term with different perspectives and renderings. When one reviews the Scriptures, it is not uncommon to realize in a chapter that there is a key term. Then, this key term is presented in different conjugations of the Arabic language or in different synonyms or other means contextualizing the case and emphasizing this concept in different parts of the chapter or even in different parts of the Scriptures. The naïve approaches of the uneducated may superficially understand this as mere repetition. Yet, the humble, educated intellectual can correspond these approaches with the new, developing fields of social and natural sciences.

OWNER'S MANUAL

One day, Rhett bought a new machine from Amazon. He was so happy and was working to assemble it by meticulously going through its manual. As he was working diligently and carefully, he was also thinking about the concept of a manual for humans. Then, he said to himself, "Yes, it is the Scriptures and other scriptures sent by God."

IN PRACTICE

God teaches us our own realities with the scriptures. In popular language, the Scriptures are the manual of a human being. They read the Scriptures in order to understand this machine-looking being with more complicated faculties of emotions, experiences, memories, concerns, worries, attachments, and reasonings. If a person takes a simple machine in order to understand its proper usage, without its manual, he or she may spend hours and still may not figure out fully its usage. On the other hand, if there is a person who makes a little bit of effort in reading the manual, that person can slowly but surely make the incremental steps of understanding and utilizing this machine. If there are any issues one can constantly go back to the manual to figure out the problems with their solutions. Similarly, the scriptures and all the prophetic teachings are the full, complete, and comprehensive manual for the person. The person constantly engages with them in order to understand their own real selves, purpose, and goal in this short lifespan. If the person acts in the illusional dispositions of self-sufficiency, the person for sure wastes all this short life with the delusions of self-experiential discoveries. All these discoveries have authentic and true value as long as they are evaluated with the principles and guidelines of these scriptural and prophetic teachings.

© Pixabay

Loss of Blessings

In its internalities, the person or the group should maintain sincerity far from group or personal identities of arrogance, wealth, knowledge, position, or title-related struggles of envy, jealousy, and motivational problems of showing off.

This positive group or personal identity should embody inclusiveness. This identity should not display the features of exclusiveness leading to arrogance. It should have the non-judgmental approaches of mysticism that any person can be a special and distinct person before the One, God, Adonai, or referred to as Allah. So, one should not break one's heart implicitly or explicitly by involving themselves with the arrogant traps of identities.

There can be a positive disposition of belonging to a group for the ones who have worldly titles, while engaging with the works of the religion. This 'belonging to' as a positive disposition can make the person desire to have the similar means such as wealth or knowledge in order to use these means effectively for the sake of God. Yet, one cannot desire the loss of this blessing from others. If one desires even a little bit the loss of this blessing of God from others, then this person indeed engages oneself with envy which can destroy the person's spirituality.

There can be a positive disposition of encouraging people to do the good by showing some role models, and by implementing best practice sharing. Yet, this should not be the essence of one's or a group's motivation as it can lead to showing off. One of the examples of show off is doing something in order to be a role model or example for others.

LOUD AND SILENT

One day, Claire attended a circle of meditation and chanting. People were chanting loudly. The next day, she attended another circle of meditation and chanting. People were chanting silently. Claire said to herself, "Wow, a person can have a choice depending on the personality and state of mind and heart at that time or day."

IN PRACTICE

There are both perspectives in loud and silent meditation and chanting. In both cases, there can be advantages. When a person is in a group of loud chanting, they can have the spiritual uplift of the audible and sensible medium. When a person is in a group of silent chanting, they can have the spiritual uplift of the sensible medium. One should remember that sometimes loud chanting can be a disadvantage due to the high pitch or loudness making it difficult for others to concentrate. As the prophets one day reminded to people, that when chanting, they should not feel the need for loudness because God is All Hearing, All Present, and Close. God is always with the person. [34][2]

Moving Forward with Sincerity

If a person or a group includes some of the spiritual diseases of the heart in their engagement of invitation or works of religion as mentioned above, then it is possible that God can replace these people or individuals with others who can work, give, and take for the sake of the One. Yet, there is always the possibility of asking forgiveness from God in all of the problematic engagements or situations.

Yet, one should remember that the people who have sincerity regardless of their small numbers should continue to work with sincerity without being discouraged due to disputes or chaos among their past or present associates.

Following the Clear Guidelines Especially at the Times of Confusion

First, one should understand, there will always be people who would engage in oppression, corruption, mischief, and chaos on the earth. Some oppression can be performed openly and overtly in the society.

Or, this chaos, conflict, and oppression plans can be executed secretly with a group and yet, these planners can claim in public that they are good wishers and they can take oaths that they are virtuous, moral, and ethical.

Yet, humans are quick to give their judgments as they take haste in life. They really make mistakes and lose etiquette and morals with God in evil-seeming incidents.

So, what do we do?

At the times of conflict or chaos, it is more important to use logic, mind, and the reason of clear guidelines as compared to the unclear guidelines of emotions.

EFFECTS OF THE SOCIETY AND HUMANNESS

Morgan as usual was practicing her life of solitude and minimal interaction with people. She sometimes used to think, "I really do not care what is happening in the world as long as I maintain my relationship with God." One day, an epidemic disease came to the world. The news about it was everywhere every day. Morgan still maintained her solitude with God without being much affected. Yet, as she was hearing the news in her minimal interaction with people, she said to herself, "As a human, it is very difficult to guard yourself from the effects of society although one can try to minimize all the social nearness."

IN PRACTICE

A person on the path is not disturbed with the daily occurrences of scandal perspectives of news. One can see a lot of people living with the news, sleeping with the news, and waking up with the news in front of them on their TVs, cell phones, and computers. They let this news navigate their emotions up and down, cracking them apart, and destroying them. Yet, a person on the path has a goal, meaning, and purpose in life. Daily occurrences or scandal news do not navigate their emotions. Therefore, the people on the path engage themselves with the useful knowledge and information as suggested by the prophets to help their lifelong goal on the path. This goal is to be happy, calm, and serene in this life by pleasing the One who is the Source of all happiness, calmness, and serenity.

Labeling, Alienation, and Promoting Conflicts

There is nothing wrong with identifying a problem. We should identify the problems in order to address them.

For example, instead of labelling or using terms that can have meanings of alienation historically such as enamored, seculars, philosophers, or academicians, one can call them people who are amazed with the rendering of the deductive reasoning, mind, and analysis, referred to as only focusing on analogical inference or deduction. Yet, balance is needed with the full method of both deductive reasoning and inductive reasoning with the etiquette and morals of the scholarly review and analysis.

For example, instead of labelling or using terms that can have meanings of alienation historically such as predecessor, literalist, or ideology followers, one can call them people who are amazed with the consensus, consensus of the pious predecessor. Yet, there must always be balance with the full method through analysis. This is critical to eliminate blind following in order to eliminate and prevent abuse and misuse and misemploy of the religious teachings through the mobilization of masses, youth, and ignorant individuals.

Rethinking our inherited terms especially in a globalized world through internet, data sharing, and immediate mass communication becomes enormously critical. Our attitudes and delivery of our knowledge referred to as methods should be constantly checked and updated in order to embody positiveness by minimizing negative judgments leading to alienation.

Attitudes of Unity and Positivity, Compassion, and Blessings

There is the reality of unification whether we realize it or not.

As a human unit, we are one. The word one can indicate this unification on a common ground despite our many differences.

Therefore, the attitudes of acceptance and tolerance promote unity and minimize the conflicts which can be the key among groups with different labels. This approach can also remind humans as the reality of being whole single unit as mentioned with the word 'one.'

This notion of positive attitude can bring compassion, merit, success, and Grace of God for the blessings and guidance of people.

Yes, unification minimizing conflicts can bring compassion. On the other hand, promotions of conflicts, separation, and isolation leading to individualist and selfish lives can bring oppression and darkness leading to negative alienation without any support.

Sometimes when a person's evil is not publicized there is a possibility that the person can stop this evil in the natural discourse of correcting oneself. Conversely, when it is publicized, there is the possibility of aggravation and increase of this evil in this person due to hate and anger of knowing that now, everyone knows publicly this person's evil.

If hypocrisy is against general human values, then it should already be against specific human values. In other words, a true faith is a trait that one can find in some groups. A person who has faith is expected to have all of the general praiseworthy human values already. A person of true faith is not expected to have hypocrisy as a trait.

From another perspective, there is an address to all of humanity that the problem of hypocrisy is a common problem. Humans can come together and solve this problem together. One can realize and understand the efforts in middle and public high schools in the West on character education. The courses of ethics and morality at highest academic level along with all the policies of academic integrity can allude to this effort of removing the bad traits of hypocrisy from humans. The curriculum of these courses perceives this as human phenomena rather than as a religious matter.

In the scriptures, one can ask: What is the philosophy behind explaining hypocrisy or hypocrites in detail with long explanations? One reason is that they may possibly stop their evil. Just like when a person gives a long lecture to a troublemaker. After that, if the person still continues, then that is the person's own fault. If especially this is a case that may affect the harmony and unity of the families, friendships, communities, and societies, then this needs to be publicized. Therefore, a long explanation style is observed to publicize their possible evil renderings so that the right choice should be clear.

In another perspective, the first reaction of the mind, intelligence of knowing can be called realization. At another level, the first reaction of ego, of true knowing can be called intuition or conscience. This first knowing of ego as conscience can be called realization of conscience. In this case, although the person can be alive, yet the faculties of conscience, the true intuition or conscience can be dead. Therefore, this first true knowing of conscience is always right and correct if it is still alive and active. In the case of hypocrites, if the conscience is dead, they cannot use this faculty to know and to implement. Ultimately, all knowledge through mind, conscience, and experience through practices should triangulate to the same result.

The below diagram shows the interpretations of feelings and knowledge through external and internal faculties.

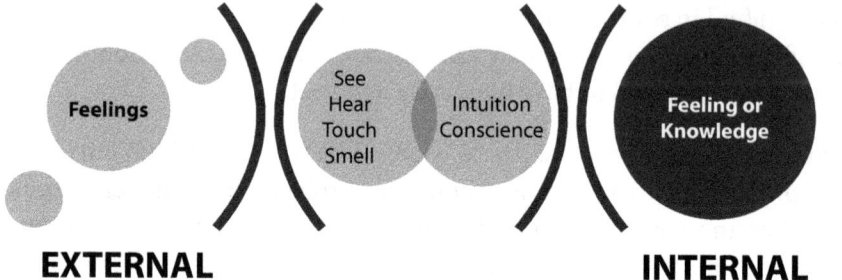

Ideally, in a natural constitution, both external and internal should be complementary and harmonizing and confirming each other in their results.

One can ask: If a person is smart in a worldly sense and one can have the above attitude, how can one reconcile the intelligence with not understanding basic premises of the true religion? A possible explanation is that when people genuinely specialize in one field, the person can also shut off oneself to other perspectives of life. In other words, a person specialized in the materialistic teachings of the seen world can very well have a minute information or no clue about the teachings of the real spiritual life and the life after death. A person who is specialized in one field still needs to have some idea and knowledge in others.

One can assume that when a person challenges another person, it is expected that there is a benefit in return for the person. The attempt of challenging God does not make any sense. There is no benefit but only harm to the person. This shows the lack of understanding and critical thinking. In other words, if a person cannot differentiate between benefit and harm, then there can be some problems either due to lack of knowledge or due to ignorance. For example, a child can touch the fire. If the child knows touching fire burns the person, then they wouldn't do it. Similarly, not being able to understand something simple such as a challenge with God can be similar to burning one's own self in the fire.

In addition, when a person does challenge, the person can expect a benefit but in reality, the person harms oneself. Every challenge can start with at least one disease of the heart such as jealousy and anger or others. If we take the case of jealousy, for example, the jealousy eats the person themselves before its harm reaches to others. In this perspective, by having this disease in one's heart, the person can go through such uncomfortable, self-rendering depressive dialogues that this person's energy is wasted and becomes a self-destructive poison. With this disease, the person constantly plans, thinks, and involves himself or herself in different, multiple versions of challenge. Yet, at the end, the person's own self is harmed.

When the person is in spiritual sickness such as in jealousy, anger, or others, the decisions made in this state can worsen the case. For example, when a person is in the state of anger, then with anger, they may do things which may make the situation worse.

Deceiving or tricking one's own self can be a sign of the lack of basic recognition, assessment, and reason.

One's own ego can be so sweet and lovely for the person that he or she will do anything to please it. However, it becomes so devastating that this lovely ego would not be able to taste the sweetness or taste with the challenge renderings of the person, but perhaps the opposite. A taste of poison affects bitterness and may be more on this earth.

The people with a spiritual disease do not understand that they are harming their own selves. Intelligence is an innate critical thinking that comes with basic recognition of harms and benefits.

THE EXTERNAL, THE INTERNAL, AND THE PURPOSE

One day, it was dark and rainy outside. Ben went to a social fitness club. As soon as he went inside, everyone was so cheerful. The lighting in the building was so bright. People were drinking coffee and enjoying their conversations at each corner. Everyone looked well dressed, happy, and smiling. Then, he thought about his solitude, loneliness, and silence. He then was reflecting on moments in the temple, or in different places of meditation. Then, he asked himself, "What is the difference?" He said: This is the external. I do not know how these people are when they are with themselves in silence, which is the internal, the real self, and, the purpose.

IN PRACTICE

It is important to know that the internal engagements are the essence that make one's purpose in life. This does not mean the person should be in gloomy environments to engage with oneself with prayers, chants, reflection, and self-accountability. The person can use all the means that would help for the real purpose when being in nature and in different environments. As in the above story, at a smaller scale, a person can be happy in a nice social club with all cheerful, fine people and places. One should know that the universe itself is a social club if one knows how to engage with it [2]. In other words, we are given a system, structure, and beings where everyone is cheering, chanting, and appreciating in their position with God. In this sense, a person not recognizing this disposition with God, may not have a real purpose although he or she may look happy. For the real sense of loneliness and self-reflection, there may be enormous internal spiritual bleeding such as depression, anxiety, and unhappiness.

DISCUSSION QUESTION

1. Who is your real self?

Religious Symbolism and Conflicts

In all of the engagements of belief, the transgressions and false approaches can occur in the over-cross of the boundaries of symbolism. In other words, one cannot reach to the essence if there is no understanding of literal versus figurative. Conversely, one can approximate to the true essence if the knowledge of boundaries is clear and distinctive. This is especially true in the spiritual journeys and in the relationship with God within the realms and tools of the human mind and experience.

If one looks at Buddhism, there is the concept of sacrifice for their sacred ones or deities. If one looks at Judaism, there is the concept of sacrifice. If one looks at Hinduism, there is the concept of sacrifice. There is the symbolic cleanliness with water or rivers. So, one can view and understand, when symbols are replaced with the essence.

In this perspective, the One is reminding to have respect for those symbols but without taking the figurative as literal. It is highly possible that God has sent similar messages for previous people but today we name them as different religions. The question is about the preservation of symbolism versus the essence.

Inter- and Intra-Religious and Non-Religious Group Interactions and Conflicts

It is possible to go beyond our group identities and interact with others. Even, this may be sometimes difficult to interact with different people within the same religious tradition.

Due to this person's ignorance, arrogance, demagogy, and lack of appreciation, the person may want to just argue. Interestingly, one may refer to this type of approach in our modern terms as 'critical thinking'. The person can miss the point if the person does not have the relevance of a holistic approach of etiquette and morals, respect, and a genuine intention to learn. Dealing with such people can be so energy draining, depressing, and self-tearing.

Conflicts Due to Diseases of the Heart

The Internal Enemy

Envy is a feeling of discontented or resentful longing aroused by someone else's given or earned possession and qualities [14].

This feeling of envy can consume the person. This consuming feeling can cause the person to have constant bad feelings about and be envious of others. The envious, consumed person can then transform their feelings into harming others by looks, words, and actions.

When the damage due to envy is done through eyes, then it is called the evil eye. This can really damage the targeted person of the envious person. One can imagine in that sense an envious person is boiling poisonous emotions in oneself. Then, its release can come through the eyes.

The second form of display of envy is through words. In this case, slandering and backbiting can be considered as some of the branching displays of envy in different forms. Generally, the person slanders and backbites the person whom they envy.

The third form of display of envy can be through actions. In this case, greed and covetousness can be some of the branching displays of envy in actions in different forms. The envious person wants to hold on to everything, be stingy, and not share in order to deprive others of the same bounty.

How to Cope with Envy

Envy generally is present with the people who understand the value of something that another person has. They get angry about it because they don't have it, but another person or people do have it.

When a person or group knows the value of anything, they have the potential of feeling envy.

If the person or group does not understand the value of something, then there may not really be envious.

The hypocrites blame the believers claiming that they are envious of them. Yet, real believers truly understand the real value of everything. They don't feel envious of the hypocrites. The level of hypocrites is so low. Envy requires knowing the real value of everything [16].

Envy and Arrogance

There is the discussion among the predecessors about the root of the spiritual diseases. According to some it is envy and jealousy and according to some it is arrogance [17]. Not going too much into this discussion of what comes first, both are explicit and very dangerous roots related with the essence of the creation of humans.

Both envy and arrogance are related. For the sake of the focus, we will try to focus here on the disease of envy, but one can also replace it and see similar approximations with the disease of arrogance in these discussions [18].

In the discussions of the predecessors, the dominant opinion seems to be that arrogance is the main source of the spiritual diseases [17]. Envy is the immediate manifestation practical application of arrogance that can be more evident and a leading force for the destruction of the person.

The manifestation of killing another person is the product of envy and arrogance.

As we are focusing on the disease of envy, it is the disease that is related with a person's strong sense of self and group identity. This identity can blind the person when something that is factual is presented to this person. Yet, the person still maintains the denial in the search and disposition of protecting this identity. Denial, lies, and false oaths are all the product and outcome of this effort of protecting this identity.

Self and ego have the free will and choice. This ability of choice can induce arrogance in the person. This free will and free choice of self induces an identity in the person. Therefore, self-identity of recognition can be the first case of manifestation of arrogance.

In other words, the person with this identity of self with the ability of making free choice can take the route of arrogance leading to self-deity.

Or, the person with this identity of self, with the ability of making free choice and executing their free will can take the route of showing off with humbleness and humility.

Yet, this is a very fine line. Its detection, struggle, or training and removal is very difficult.

Ability of choice has a natural tendency to indulge in arrogance like an animal who wants to wander without a leash. Holding this animal with the leash and directing to the allowed and permissible path requires effort, struggle, and constant engagement with the animal.

Similarly, our own selves with free will and choice is like that animal that needs to have the leash not to go to the impermissible lawns of arrogance. That is not our lawn [7] [19].

In this regard if arrogance is not detected and trained, then the second immediate soldier of arrogance who is envy, is waiting to attack, and transfuse, in emotions, thoughts, and ideas. Then, the next step is displaying these actions with evil.

In this regard, every envy can be due to arrogance. Arrogance is difficult to detect. Envy is easier to detect because envy is the manifestation of the arrogance in the person's thoughts and emotions leading to actions.

Yes, we have different tendencies, emotions, and thoughts. The main goal of our test is to constantly, but constantly, gauge them in allowed actions and permissible fields, lawns, and areas of engagement. Envy is the trunk and the branches of the root of the arrogance.

Removing the root of the arrogance is the lifelong struggle and gist of the secrecy of life.

Envy is the trunk and branch of the root of arrogance. The person may not see the invisible root under the ground, but they can see the trunk and branches above the ground.

Envy and Its Display

One can review envy as a display of arrogance in our actions. If arrogance is the intention, then envy is its action.

The true healthy person has faith, religion, and sincerity. [20].

The diseased person has arrogance, envy, and like an embodiment of the devil.

The display of one's faith is through religion. The display of one's arrogance is true envy.

Or, with their free choice and free will, they can be in the valleys of negativity with arrogance.

WINNERS AND LOSERS

One day, Jax gained a lot of knowledge, piety, and respect. He started to have a lot of followers changing themselves with his teachings on the path of God. Jax's friends and family members were also benefiting from his knowledge and teachings. They said to themselves, "We are so lucky that we have Jax in our lives. What a great bounty of God! It is like winning a lottery!" Yet, a few of his old friends and family members got jealous and said, "Why him? We are better than Jax. Why don't people follow us, but they follow him?" They have become increasingly jealous of him. They lost on the path of winning.

IN PRACTICE

It is important to detect our spiritual diseases before they spiritually kill us. A person on the path of God can be winning yet he or she can lose with jealousy. Satan is the primary example of this. On the other hand, an intelligent person can realize that if God chooses some people to be the role models such as the prophets, and saints, then an intelligent person can make use of this to benefit their own spiritual growth. An intelligent person benefits from the people who are the source of light and guidance as the friends of God. Spiritually killing oneself with jealousy and self-destructive hatred is the worst foolishness, absurdity, and irrationality. When one reviews the life of the prophets, everyone boosted their true spirituality with their pearl and diamond teachings. Yet, there were a few from their old friends and family members who blocked themselves due to their iron curtains built with jealousy, hatred, and arrogance in their hearts.

Envy and Identities

Arrogance as a disease can make the person blind and deaf when there is a reality, factual, reasonable, and logical case presented. Yet, the arrogant does not hear or see any of them although the presenter may be constantly talking and showing different perspectives to prove their factual and reasonable point.

When this self with arrogance situates themselves in a group, this attitude of arrogance embedded in self-identity transforms itself to the attitude of arrogance embedded in a group identity. Yet, although one can see a group as a unit together with this disingenuous motivation of arrogance, the matters of self and the self as an individual are in shattered states.

In this regard, these diseased individuals with arrogance carrying these group identities do not accept anything or anyone unless they have the ID card of their group. As mentioned, being in that group is just a vehicle or tool of the manifestation of this diseased self in the group.

In any group, not all of the individuals are the same, some may have arrogance. While others can be genuine and sincere.

These genuine ones are the people whom when they are presented some factual data, logical and plausible approaches, they don't deny them. They immediately go back to their real self as individuals beyond their group identities to decode who they are with humbleness and humility.

Today, one can call this true open-mindedness, acceptance, tolerance, and being scientific and civilized.

The approach of the revelations is not to instruct the person or individuals to change identities, fans, clubs, or group associations. The revelations are simply, clearly, and genuinely advising to consider logical, plausible, and reasonable approaches with fairness and justice.

Envy goes further. It desires the person to lose what they have, suffer, and be in pain.

The people of envy do not agree, accept, or act to be open-minded, unless the person or individual leaves their group and goes to another group.

In other words, sometimes our group identities fueled by our individual, self-related, arrogant identities make us forget the principles and purpose of being in that group.

Therefore, healthy groups are formed by healthy individuals. The person who is in a group should constantly go always back to their healthy individual state to check if the person is in line with the group principles or guidelines compared to the people who are practicing these teachings.

Yes, there may be some changes and updates as details of deep and comprehensive understanding adapted by scholars can indicate. Yet, these are details as agreed to in the origins of consensus of the scholars of the majority in those emerging problems with their solutions. Similarly, one can find the similar dispositions in different religions.

When a case is presented, the person can do this self-check or alignment according to their healthy self-using their mind, without arrogance.

The Stains of the Heart and Chest

When we engage with others, we tend to have some feelings that may make us uncomfortable. These negative feelings can emerge immediately in the person after the person remembers an incident or memory, talks or sees another individual. Sometimes, it can be related when the person hears something. Sometimes, it may reveal itself when the person passes by a place. The symptoms of these feelings can be discomfort, a feeling bothering from internal senses, uneasiness, or immediate change of state of peace into some problematic disturbed internal states. Sometimes, these feelings last a few seconds, sometimes hours, and sometimes days.

These engagements can give stamina to the person with the merit and Grace of the One to maintain patience and to unshackle oneself from the detrimental effects and results of these disturbing internal feelings.

Sometimes, the person can do a purposeful seclusion detaching oneself from people so that the person does not hurt others under the control of these negative feelings.

If these feelings emerge when the person interacts with another person, then the person should try to detect the problem and why or how these negative feelings defined as resentment form so that in similar situations, the person can possibly train oneself.

The person should look at their spiritual diseases and then, detect the specific problem in oneself as the contextualized case of resentment. For example, while the person was in interaction with another individual, did the person feel that he did not receive much of the deserved respect while talking or communicating with this person? Did the person feel that the other person was arrogant or haughty? Did the person feel that a trust was broken when the other individual exposed the secrets of this person? These questions with our assumptions, whether true or false, can go further.

Yet, if we analyze these questions with the principles of mysticism, then everything should be taken as a self-reflection point as a problem of spiritual disease in the person but not in the other person. For example, getting frustrated due to the feelings of undeserved or poor or low treatment can be a sickness of superiority in the person themselves rather than on the other person. This can be relevant and beneficial knowledge for the self to know and accordingly work on themselves.

Sometimes, we may not understand the source of this comfort mentioned as resentment. Yet, this can be a problem or a disease that the person may need to identify its source and work on it.

Today, we may refer to these sicknesses as judgment of others. The spiritual sickness of judgment, as taught in mysticism, can be branching out from jealousy, envy, and arrogance.

In this perspective, resentment, is a disease or stain of the heart. One can understand the effect and result of this disease in the afterlife.

The gist of the creation is sincerity. Sincerity is very difficult to achieve and maintain. To achieve the state of sincerity one should be aware of all of one's inner renderings, engagements, feelings, and thoughts. Accordingly, one can take necessary actions. To be in the station of sincerity, one should maintain this constant and continuous inner-self check and take the necessary corrective actions.

When a feeling comes bothering the person and making him uncomfortable, the person should immediately indulge in taking care of it, self-inner check, to identify the source of the problem. Sometimes, identifying the problems can take a second, sometimes a minute, sometimes an hour, sometimes days, and sometimes years. Yet, it is possible that without proper identification, there won't be any proper action.

One should remember that the purpose of achievement, striving, and struggle is called purification, sanctification, or decontamination of the self or ego, because the ego is filled with diseases and filth.

Every ego has its own world filled with filth, garbage, and spiritual urine which are disgusting and lowly engagements for the soul.

This filth is so disgusting that the Creator gave humans the cover of externality with the physical body. No one knows the reality, essence, and internal core of this inner world of the person. Most of the time, the person himself or herself may not even know their own inner world of the realities.

Yes, every person has a spiritual world bigger than this physical earth that we are living in. This world smells, is repulsive, and disgusting if not sanctified and purified.

Distorted—The World of Filthy Self

This filthy state of the world of the person can be called 'stinginess'.

This world has the elements of selfishness, egotism, stinginess, and arrogance. Dark air mixes with the poisonous plants of jealousy, fruits of greed, anger, and vanity along the pathways of lies. This world is always dark. There is no daylight. The atmosphere is always dark without any sky but with dark, depressive and scary fogs.

Yet, our world or my world is not different than others unless there is the process of constant cleansing through first acceptance, or realization. Then, cleaning with seeking forgiveness from the One and relating oneself with the Pure.

This process is the essence of life and living.

Yet, the process of cleansing of this filth first starts with stopping oneself intentionally, and purposefully due to fear of God as this can be called forbearance, fear, and abstinence.

With the initial stage and practices of forbearance, fear, and abstinence one can go to the higher stages of pleasure of God.

In this perspective this is the world of the raw, unfiltered self that needs purification.

HEART DISEASES AND DETECTION

One day, Chloe was praying in a park. Her kids were playing. There was another family and a small girl. Chloe gave one candy to all her children. Her kids came and asked her for seconds, and she said, "No." Then, a small girl came to Chloe and asked for a candy. She gave her a candy. Then, after the girl finished her candy, she came and asked for another one. Chloe was thinking, "What should I say? I have a few more candies left. They are expensive." Chloe told the small girl to wait. She was looking in her bag to see if she can give something else to the small girl. Realizing this, the small girl's mother came and got very angry at the small girl. She felt horrible and said to herself, "My stinginess!"

IN PRACTICE

Like the above story, Chloe immediately tried to detect her spiritual disease in the incident instead of blaming the mother. In spiritual endeavors, it is a level to know one's own spiritual disease. Then, one can work on his or her disease. Stinginess is a disease that sometimes may be hard to detect. Stinginess is a sign of attachment which can be the opposite of the positive spiritual state of detachment. For every positive spiritual state, there can be an opposite state as a spiritual disease.

DISCUSSION QUESTION

1. Is it difficult to detect one's own spiritual diseases? Why?

Different Worlds of Ego and Heart

The world of raw and unfiltered ego is the world of stinginess [21]. In this world of the self, when there is purification, the ego starts realizing the intrinsic diseases of the heart referred to as stains or diseases of the heart.

Expectations, Disappointments, and the Formation of Physiological or Psychological Sickness

Here, one can try to identify the process of a sickness- the existing stage, its development, and metastasis until one dies. One can ask how the worsening of a sickness can occur.

In one possible case of humanly engagement, if a person expects a lot from another person but cannot get what he or she desires to receive, then the person can get upset. Over the course of time, with this agitation, the person gets disappointed in this other person whom he or she claims to love a lot, and begins to question the relationship with this person. Over the course of time with agitation, and disappointment, the person can move to the next stage of unimaginable anger. With this increasing anger, the next stage can start with hate.

When a person is in the disposition of anger and hate, it is very difficult to expect reason, logic, and rationale. Now, at this position, the person becomes spiritually and mentally sick.

One can see that the disease of lying becomes part of their natural constitution and character. They lie so much that lying becomes part of their traits. They lie but they don't consider lying to be a lie or to be evil. Furthermore, they consider lying, deceiving, and related engagements with marketing or politics as a positive and virtuous trait to achieve their goals. They lie in political life to deceive people. They lie in executive manners to force others to follow their instructions. They lie in social affairs to manipulate massive crowds and nations.

It is also interesting to see that since these people lie; they think that others lie too. This is a sickness. They demonstrate the highest level of skepticism and distrust due to their position of continuous lying. With this psychology, they constantly think that people constantly plot against them.

When a person starts lying, then it becomes a very difficult path from which to come back [7] [22]. One can always reflect on the trait of lying both in personal affairs and social and political affairs. In the sociological phenomena of group dynamics, lying can be painted with the notions of achieving something good. However, religion does not approve of achieving a high goal with the means of unethical and immoral paths. One should also remember that the affairs that are based on lies can possibly engulf the liars one day with different social and personal dynamics and incidents.

One can also analyze the social effects of lying and truthfulness in the societies in relation to the decline or advancement of civilizations. One can examine the societies where lying and all related social discourses is the dominant norm and how the societies can be poor, backwards, and unhappy. Conversely, one can also examine societies where lying is not very prevalent as compared to others and how this disposition affects and helps the advancement of civilization and prosperity in these societies.

As lying is a major disease of the heart, another disease mentioned here is the negative group identities or identity.

One can ask: What is the philosophy behind detailing the characters of hypocrites? First, in the encounters of life, a person will encounter people with different backgrounds, motifs, and intentions. One of the difficult ones to understand is the hypocrite. They externally proclaim to be with you, but when they actually are not, a naïve person can be confused by this type of stance.

The second philosophy can be to normalize the existence of these people and not to be frustrated by their engagements. Much of the time when humans cannot categorize or identify the reasons, they may get frustrated and hopeless. Therefore, the explanations can help the person to normalize the existence of such a group of people.

If one looks at the definition of the word 'disease' in Oxford dictionary, it is "a disorder of structure or function in a human, a particular quality, habit, or disposition regarded as adversely affecting a person or group of people." [23] In this perspective, a person with this trait cannot differentiate between the right and wrong, or authentic and false. This disease can be solidified in a hypocrite and a denier.

These diseases can be inside the depths of their hearts so that it can be very difficult to identify, reveal, and treat.

In addition, a person is born with a natural, healthy state of heart and mind referred to as 'natural constitution' in terminology. If God created everyone with a sound heart or a natural constitution, then this means that in their hearts, there is a type of disease that had damaged this original state. This state is earned and an acquired state with one's disposition, tendency, and free choice in life. So, no one can blame any person other than themselves in this regard. One can review the previous discussions about the concepts of person's acquirement in terminology.

It is difficult to define or diagnose this sickness or disease. It can be difficult for the person who has the disease to know and diagnose it. It can also be difficult for others to understand that when they interact with this person that this person has a disease.

On another perspective, one can interpret the root of this disease to be at the heart. It metastasizes to other parts of the body such as the mind, eyes, or ears [7].

The punishment reveals itself due to mainly the sickness of lying. Lying, the opposite of honesty, is such a bad trait that it hurts the person immediately if the person still has some portions of a sound and healthy heart and conscience. These feelings can make the person constantly doubtful, uneasy, stressful, and anxious. This in itself is an immediate punishment, let alone the expected punishment in the afterlife. Conversely, if a person is in honesty and truthfulness, this makes the person very firm, clear, and peaceful. There are not complications of mismatch of verbal utterances with the internal heart and conscience-related renderings. They both match with each other. In the case of a liar, there is always the complicated process of normalizations of outward affairs of words and actions with the inward affairs of intentions, and feelings.

One should remember that health is the default state of a person. Sickness is an exception. Sometimes, a virus can make the person sick. If the person does not care about this virus, then it can grow and spread. Something trivial can become major and kill the person. Similarly, a virus of doubt can come to the person with the matters of the religion. In this sense, if a person does not take care of this virus immediately, this trivial virus can grow and spread in such a way that the person can become a non-believer. In this sense, increase of sickness is due to the person's fault. At the end, the person should blame themselves.

One should realize that there could be different levels of lying in each person's life. The important part here is to regret and ask forgiveness from God in each possible case of lying renderings. A true believer is expected to actively take constant care of one's relationship with God. In other words, they always see himself or herself as the oppressor, committing injustice against oneself. Because, one cannot truly appreciate God until they understand that they are an oppressor. In other words, appreciating or being grateful to God requires embodying and personalizing that one cannot truly accomplish thanking God. Embodying and personalizing this attitude as a trait is the main step on the true path of God. In all of these discussions, the people who are in the group are on the opposite pole. They are not even aware of the bounties of God and they are not aware of their own selves.

Any type of disease related with the heart is considered dangerous because the heart is a critical organ for the body. This can allude to the fact and notion that this disease is extremely serious, hidden, and deep inside the layers but not something easy to recognize, understand, and handle.

A healthy heart will require a sound faith. In this perspective, the Scriptures first and foremost reveal the importance of the main disease in the heart. If the essence is sound and healthy, then one can focus on the details such as the health of the body. A heart with sound faith will have a positive effect on the health of the body. However, if the spiritual heart of the person is sick, then it is going to have an effect on the physical heart. Then, all of the body, mind, and the person will suffer due to this. In this perspective, the word metastasis, the spread of the disease from its core to other places in the body, takes place.

The natural state of a human is both physically and spiritually to be healthy. Sickness is not the essence but is an auxiliary state. Similarly, corruption and destruction are an auxiliary sickness. No one claims to have this state permanently. Therefore, claims of a hypocrite to be in this state permanently is solely their fault and no one else's.

Lies and Show Off

The person oppresses his or her own self. They have been oppressing their own selves, egos, bodies in this world and in the afterlife.

According to some scholars, the pronoun 'I' is dangerous to use. Someone's utterances and expressions of 'my work', 'I did this....' can be examples of this implicit oppression (injustice). On the contrary, all the destructions, evils, and bad outcomes are from the self, ego, and the person. The person asks for it and then it is created for this person.

Killing as an Outcome of Spiritual Disease

One can analyze two cases around the word and concept of a familial relationship, brotherhood, or sisterhood. In the first case, there is no destructive jealousy but helping each other to save themselves both from the displeasure of God. This is encouraged and it is a positive kinship relationship when one is helping another.

On the other hand, consider the case of two brothers. One shows jealousy, attitude and injustice, and the other shows humbleness, and forbearance, fear and abstinence. They are both kinship brothers. The jealousy presents itself at such a level that the oppressor kills the innocent. One brother kills the other.

The first one is the ideal case as a role model. A positive kinship relationship can grant the person blessings in this world and in the afterlife. The second case is the one in which humans tend to make a bad or wrong choice due to the diseases of the heart, ego, and temptations of the devil.

People are in a state of delusion due to their urges and desires they want to do what they want to do in a blind state.

It is interesting to control one's urges such as anger, lust, or others. They can possibly make the person blind if the person does not control or gauge them in positive and permissible ways.

One can see that in the cases or states of blindness, the person cannot differentiate right from wrong or experiences blurriness. Another time that puts the person in an utmost mixture of delusion, confusion, or blindness is at the time of death.

One of the important methodologies of the Scriptures is that they teach us the importance of narration. This can be translated as contextualization of meanings, theorizations through religious disciplines of creed, and religious disciplines of law. The reason to especially emphasize this point is the expectation regarding people of the book.

One can clearly and amazingly see another miracle of the Scriptures with the piece-by-piece revelations, and then rearrangement of these contextualizations through narration with their inclusion in chapters and the arrangement of these chapters, and then the final compilation as a book. This is the methodology taught to us by God.

In today's discipline of social studies, an arguable reality is that everything has a context. From this contextualization, case studies, generalizations, and theories develop to span across space and time. Across space and time means in this case, across the Arabs, countries, regions, ethnicities, age groups and generations, and centuries. This is a current methodology that our modern scientific academic institution has fully adapted today. Yet, this was there and given to us 1600 years ago by God.

Yet, in this sense of the methodology, the Scriptures break the solid boundaries between revelation, reason, mind, and experience through the methodology of contextualization referred to as 'reason revelation'. In other words, if the Scriptures were revealed in the form of tablets as the revelation, then the mind and experience distinction can be more clearly reflected on the social norms belonging only to those times and spaces of revelation.

Yet, the existence of 'reason revelation' is another proof for the universality, flexibility, adaptability, and contextualization of the Scriptures for all times and spaces. There is no book or scripture after the Scriptures because there is no need for a new book.

Yet, the Scriptures with the narration build up all the teachings from real cases with critical thinking, reasoning, experience of mind and heart in order to reflect the social norms of relevance in our times and spaces which will be valid until the Day of Judgment.

On another note, as one can start reading the Scriptures, one can clearly realize this continuity in that all the meanings, flow, context, verses, and chapters are bound together. This is as if it is one piece. It is one single time revelation. It is one tablet. It is very difficult to assign classical stop signs such as comma, period or other differentiating the topics in a true sense.

In other words, contextualization reveals our humanness. As humans, we may have a limited capacity to bear and engage with the Scriptures as a whole, entire piece. God mentions in the Scriptures this human reality and their engagement with the Scriptures and yet, a person can still receive the benefit of the Scriptures if he or she reads a few verses from the Scriptures.

On the other hand, God also reminds of the people who are elect but can try to embody the revelation of the Scriptures as a single piece and they cannot stop reading until they finish the Scriptures.

One can ask: Why are the Scriptures deemed the greatest miracle of the prophets?

There are very simple, easy, and straightforward answers to this question.

First, this is the book of God. Being the last book requires no need for any other scriptures from God. If there are no more scriptures from God, then the Scriptures should be preserved, and remain authentic and original until the Day of Judgment. God promises and gives us the covenant that the Scriptures will not change and will be authentic and original until the End of Days. In other words, the preservation of the Scriptures is by the Divine Assurance.

One of the reasons for different scriptures being sent by God is due to the changes and alterations of the original messages in these scriptures. If the Scriptures will not be changed and will be authentic, then there is no need for another scripture. The Scriptures are fully satisfactory and sufficient.

Second, a miracle as a teaching lasts just a few seconds, a few minutes, hours, or mostly days to bring people back into the realities of truth. In this sense, miracles from God can make enormous transformations in people instantly and permanently as one can witness this with magicians going through this change when they encountered the true miracles.

A Book that is sent from the Creator, original and authentic, and that explains all of our purposes, our selves, knowns and unknowns is a gigantic miracle!

When there is a miracle, that does not last for a few seconds, a few minutes or a few days, but lasts a thousand years or until the end of the human journey, then this is in itself an enormous miracle, mercy, and graciousness from God.

In other words, if the prophets are the messengers of God until the End of Days, then there should be a teaching or something that would counter and remind these laws of God if there is a need. With the Graciousness, Justice, and Mercy of God, God gives the Scriptures to us as a permanent teacher until the End of Days.

Accessibility of this miracle, and availability of this miracle at all times to everyone is another miracle.

This is all from the graciousness and mercy of God.

PHRASES ON THE TONGUE

Violet used to memorize divine phrases and parts of the Scriptures in their original language of revelation. She was trying to understand the meanings but sometimes she did not understand the meanings, and yet still memorized it. One day, she was sleeping and woke up with one of the words that she had memorized and found that she was repeating it involuntarily. She looked up the meaning of the word that she was repeating and said to herself, "Aha! That is the answer. Now everything makes sense."

IN PRACTICE

Divine phrases and verses from the Scripture can embody different beings and can help the person in different parts of life difficulties. When the person appreciates God and all the divine phrases and the Scripture from God, they can act like a superman to save the person in the times of need. It is kind of a payback time. When the person needs help, these divine phrases and good deeds can come and save this person. No good deed goes into nothingness, it has a life of its own, in this life and the next. This is a common belief across the tradition. Each phrase, chant, prayer, and recitation of the scripture can take different forms to help the person in this world and in the afterlife. There are narrations that the five-times prayers of a person can come in the form of a human being after the person's death in the grave or on Judgment Day and can comfort the person from all worries. When the person sees this unknown person the person asks, "Who are you?" and this unknown person replies, "I am your prayers that you used to pray. Now, it is my turn to help you."

Observation and Analysis

In other words, the above process of change is observable by almost all humans. Why do the Scriptures mention that they are for us? There can be many reasons. Among many, here are some possibilities.

<u>Normalization:</u> A person witnesses and experiences this change of weakness and a needy disposition as a baby, then acquires strength and an independent stance in the ages of youth and adulthood, and becomes again weak and needy in the old age of senility. What does this mean? If the person does not know or acquire a proper meaning of this reality, then it is very easy and possible that the person can become depressed, anxious, and miserable.

There are some changes happening in one's body and faculties of mind, yet the person is only observing it but cannot do anything about it and does not have any control over it. God created this process and it is normal. It is something out of the control of humans. There are a lot of things in our lives that are out of our control although we may claim that we own it. For example, we are not in control of biological cells and how they are working and what they are doing in our body. We are not in control of our organs made up of these cells and how they are working and what they are doing, such as our liver, kidney, gallbladder, spleen and others in our body. We are not in control of our physiological systems made up by these organs and how they are working and what they are doing such as our nervous system, circulatory system, hormonal glands, and others in our bodies. Yet, we all claim to own them as our body. God as the God maintains them. Similarly, changes in our bodies as we age is something out of our control. God mentions in the Scriptures that this is a reality as part of our creation.

Once, the person expects and knows that this is coming, then there are minimal feelings of depression, anxiety, and misery so that we don't feel that we are losing something that we own such as our strength, our hair, our teeth, our sight, our movement abilities, and others.

At our present time, the cases of scheduling, or preparations for the events are the means of human psychology in order to establish a lifestyle that is able to prevent stressful, random, immediate, or instant occurrences of change. Therefore, unexpected losses in one's life such as death, accidents, or others have very devastating effects because the person is not prepared for them. In this regard of preparation, God explains these observable and scheduled events in a human's life so that the person should be ready for these changes mentally, and spiritually. Accordingly, they should make preparation for it.

Accessibility of Common Observable Events: The other important point is that God gives these normalization points with common observable events that take place in the Scriptures. In this stance, one can be deceived and take these observable events for granted and move on in one's life. Or another can realize these meanings and purpose, and he or she may not take those for granted. Examples include the cases of rain, wind, air, trees, stones, sky, earth, mountains, spouses, social incidents, and many other observable events by humans mentioned in the Scriptures in many places. Yet, one can take the disposition of stating that everything is explainable with science. In this case, the person is being curtained by the immediate layer but not going through the essence or purpose. Therefore, the Scriptures or a scripture sent by God is not a technical or expert book in the immediate meaning but accessible to everyone although the scholars can derive a lot of meanings with their expertise. Religion is accessible to everyone.

Need for a True Authority of Meanings: There should be an authority who should explain these meanings. If there are more than five billion people on the earth, everyone can have an idea about these meanings. Yet, an Authority not in our dimension or realm should tell us the consolidating, true, and objective meanings. This authority is the Scripture revealed by our Creator, God.

Different Meanings of the Scriptures for Different Stakeholders/ Human Types: Each verse of the Scriptures can have different meanings for different people amongst different age, social, ethnic, cultural, and economic backgrounds in different times of human history.

Before you die, you will return to your weak state of mental and physical faculties. This is a last chance for you to be humble in front of your Creator if you are a denier before you meet with your Creator. This last stage of weakness is a hope and glad tidings for a believer that you will soon meet with your Creator that you have been longing for all of your life.

Method of Learning

It is important to understand that the Scriptures explain the realities related with belief and knowing God in detail [24]. From another perspective, God makes science and scientific explanations in nature available in detail in order for people to reach knowledge about belief and its realities with knowing the names of God.

Our free will with free choice indicates and leads to using our inclinations to convince our own selves. This is a lifelong struggle. It does not and may not often happen immediately.

If God had wished, a sign or a verse could have made all humans fully submit to God.

Yet, this is not the purpose and goal.

One can understand the knowledge about the oneness of God in Dedicating all acts to God as the authentic, true knowledge that is bestowed on us through the Scriptures and Actions of the prophets. In this sense, we humbly submit, follow, and accept. The key term, 'submission', can be critical in this case in that we must submit ourselves humbly to the truth as religious people.

One can make an analogy of this in the methodology of natural and social sciences and humanities as inductive reasoning. Inductive reasoning is characterized by the extrapolation of general laws to particular cases [12]. It is the methodology of understanding by having general laws or principles as the primary approach to understanding. In sociology, one may call this macro-analysis of policy making. In education, one may call this a top-down approach as opposed to the grounded theory. When something becomes a scientific word, no one questions its validity, but people accept this new law. They use this law to understand another phenomenon.

On the other hand, it can be possible to view the knowledge about the oneness of God as the authentic, true knowledge that is bestowed on us through our daily and constant experience and conscience. In this case, one may try to get a meaning to construct, build, and struggle to build until one dies. The key term struggle can be critical in this case to remember. It is a constant struggle, until one dies, to correctly connect the pieces to have certainty in the oneness of God through Creations of God. In this sense, the word belief can be critical in that one struggles and tries to establish the certainty in Religion through experiential knowledge and witnessing of knowledge until one dies.

One can make an analogy of this in the methodology of social and natural sciences and in the humanities as is similar to deductive reasoning. Deductive reasoning is characterized by the extrapolation of particular cases to arrive at general laws [14]. It is the methodology of understanding each piece and experience constantly and relentlessly. In sociology, one may call this micro-analysis of policy making. In education, one may call this grounded theory. In anthropology or philosophy, one may call this phenomenology. The engagements of mysticism, experiential and experimental knowledge, can all be under the category of this approach. One can reach to the true oneness of God with Creations of God.

Therefore, the staging of religion to belief can be related to oneness of God in dedicating all acts to God.

In a true religion, both inductive and deductive reasonings, scriptural knowledge bestowed on us, and our experiential and mind-related constant struggle until we die, should be expected to triangulate to the same fact and reality. In other words, all engagements of oneness of God in Dedicating all acts to God and Creations of God show the same result of true oneness of God.

The Name of God as The Unique can indicate the Oneness of God in Dedicating all acts to God.

Etiquette and Morals of Learning

In this regard, a good teacher can explain in detail the questions.

Yet, etiquette and morals of learning and questioning are always related with the people's intentions in learning. In other words, questioning for the sake of challenging or arrogance is an attitude without etiquette and morals.

Although it is difficult to maintain the composure at these times if someone is teaching, yet one should still not assume but make their best effort to teach without any judgment especially during our times of Western dominance where constant questioning is promoted and encouraged as a norm.

It is important to teach the manners of etiquette and morals to children in learning, questioning, and other etiquette in interaction as our successful precedors implemented and embodied as inspired by the Scriptures and Actions of the prophets.

Learning without etiquette and morals can generate people and youth to become pumped up with fake arrogance far from our values of etiquette and morals. The individualistic societies in the West are the natural outcome of these pseudo-inspired self-sufficient individuals with confidence.

Learning with etiquette and morals can generate people and youth who can plant seeds of generations and youth who themselves can maintain inner peace with their own selves and others. The social life in Eastern cultures besides many of their problems is still the natural outcome of these remnant teachings of etiquette and morals in these societies.

LEARNING WITH THE CHILDREN

One day, Alia was studying with her children. She gave some studying materials to them. At first, the kids whined about the work. As they continued studying, they got excited about learning and discovering the unknown realities on their own. Alia as a teacher knew all of the answers to the questions that she was trying to teach. As the lessons continued, she was amazed about the reaction of the kids and their satisfaction due to learning by struggle. Alia said to herself, "If I gave the answers from the beginning, they would not learn this well, and would not enjoy and appreciate the knowledge." She said to herself, "This is similar to the tests, trials, and struggles to self-witness one's actions and come closer to God until one dies."

IN PRACTICE

It is important to realize that God knows everything, future and the past. One of the secrets of life is that God creates humans to self-witness their own journey in their relationship with God. Thus, humans cannot claim otherwise in front of God after death.

DISCUSSION QUESTION

1. Why do people tend to appreciate their own effort of self-discoveries as compared to outcomes or achievements given without much effort?

Etiquette and Morals as Reminders of our Limits

Impossibilities challenge and remind us of our limits as humans. The technical word in the discipline for this challenging perspective of the Scriptures to all humans, Other Spirits, and the rest of creation can be referred to as 'challenge'.

In other words, Scriptures teach and remind us of our limits as humans and all creation in front of God. One can also refer to this as knowing our etiquette and morals as servants of God.

Sometimes, if a person goes out of etiquette and morals, and others still maintain niceness with this person, then this person's oppression and transgression may increase due to normalizing or not realizing the absence of his or her etiquette and morals. Therefore, it can be critical to remind of everyone's limits in human relations if the limits are transgressed.

Nowadays, terminologies like, professionalism, and professional distance at work, absence of abuse, absence of oppression at home, and absence of bullying among peers can all be new forms or expressions of morals. In other words, the policies, guidelines, and teachings are set to remind people of their limits in relationships to maintain respectful and healthy relationships.

The notion of etiquette and morals are in that sense knowing everyone's limits in their relationships with others. When we analyze the same approach in our relation with God, most of the problems of theodicy—the vindication of God in the presence of evil—alienation, or isolation from religion stem from the absence of etiquette and morals with God. There may be explicit and implicit involvements of absent etiquette and morals with God whether it is through actions, words, thoughts, or emotions.

We can take the Scriptures and the prophets as our role models in our lives to know our limits. We can learn the true etiquette and morals from the Scriptures and actions of the prophets.

In normal cases of difficulties and challenges, one can say it is my personal incapacity. But, if it is something for all humans and creation that none can do anything about, then the person and all humans, who have the option of choice and free will, should really pause and reconsider their objective stance.

This can also be similar to expected positions about a global problem that God may shake all humans with their possible false renderings of refuge or explicit/implicit associating others with God. For example, pandemic diseases such as the Covid-19 virus can be one of the latest examples of this challenge given by God from another perspective. All of the means can seem to pause.

These divine reminders as global challenges can be the means for us to realize who we are in reality, what our goal is, and how and what we are doing towards these goals.

Attitudes, Behavior, and Religion

The Process of Formation of Doubts

The lower self can always tend to approach the teachings and examples of the Scriptures with the darkness of disbelief. Accordingly, it does not understand the wisdom of these examples. Due to the tendency of the spiritual sickness in the heart [25], any doubt or question can become so important and so critical as if they become the essence and pillar of the religion. Then, naturally, the person loses the right path, the truth as invaded with the doubts in the heart and mind. Then, this person starts asking questions. Still, he or she cannot find a solution to his or her doubts. Then, he or she starts denial, disbelief, unappreciation, ungratefulness of pessimism and darkness referred to as disbelief.

Humbleness, humility, and reliance on God with trust in God's plan are the key elements to be safe as a life vest. When the person trusts in himself or herself even for the size of an atom, then this can for sure be the point of loss and a turning point to darkness and pessimism. The real power, light, calmness, serenity, peace and tranquility is in full and all trust in God.

RELIANCE ON GOD

Anya had a very personal and close relationship with God. Whatever she asked from God, God gave her exactly what she wanted. One day, she lost her job. She was afraid that if she asked God, God would give her exactly what she wanted. Then, she said to herself, "I will show reliance on God and pray for whatever God chooses to give for me. I am happy as long as God is pleased with me."

> **IN PRACTICE**
>
> It is important to reach the level of reliance in practice. Most of the time when evil happens, we tend to blame people or God and ruin our relationships. In the above story, Anya had a very close relationship with God through constant prayer and appreciation. Therefore, God always gave her what she wanted in life. She reached one of the highest levels of reliance called *tawakkul*. In this stage, all the evil or good-looking incidents are the same for the person as long as God is pleased with that person.

Attitudes Leading to Belief or Disbelief

Attitude is the final and ultimate cause and reason of one's guidance, leading to belief, misguidance, or disbelief.

God can guide and misguide any person. In other words, guidance is with the Mercy, Graciousness, and Grace of God due to showing inclinations of humbleness and humility on the path of God.

Misguidance and ending up in disbelief are the attitude of a disbeliever and a depraved person. Anyone that has a miniscule or atom size tendency even in their thoughts or emotions to blame God for the misguidance will therefore, due to their free will, acquisition, end up in disbelief and misguidance from their choice.

The attitude of belief necessitates humbleness and humility of submission that whatever God mentions, they know that that is the truth. They may try to understand the wisdom in these teachings to increase their certainty about knowing the names of God. Yet, their initial attitude is not to object, to question, or implicitly make fun like a disbeliever or a person that says they are a believer but is not.

When one analyzes the responses of the disbeliever or a person that says they are a believer but is not in the Scriptures, one can realize this initial and immediate position of objection, questioning, and arrogance as their display of disbelief and misguidance.

The primary example of this is Satan when he was ordered to prostrate to Adam. He did not fulfill it but questioned it. Then, in this attitude his followers follow Satan and Other Spirits.

Conversely, the people of belief have the initial and immediate position of humbleness and humility for any teaching coming from God with acceptance, submission, and following.

Angels, when ordered to prostrate before Adam fulfilled the order although they had a question about etiquette and morals for God about the creation of Adam.

The choice of Attribute and Name of God shows the intrinsic disposition of proximity, sincerity, and humbleness and humility of the people of belief in their hearts and minds in actualizing the commands and teachings of God.

One can possibly say that God gives these examples in the Scriptures to differentiate the intrinsic attitudes of people. These examples can serve the purpose of a test or a trial to differentiate the different levels, the passing and the failing, the pure and the filthy, the humble and the arrogant.

The Scriptures are for the guidance of the person. Yet, with this general rule, one should always remember that a beneficial item can always be harmful for some exceptional people if they often misuse the general purpose of this item or if they have a wrong or improper intention of using this item.

For a thirsty person may want to eat a cold watermelon. If there is knife, one can cut this big watermelon and can benefit from the usage of this knife. Yet, if the same person uses the same knife to harm a person, then it is not used in its proper usage. Then, it becomes depraved, a misuse leading to chaos and self-destruction.

In this regard, the Scriptures immediately explain this exceptional position. The people who have the problem of depravation can actually destroy themselves if they have the wrong intention and attitude.

This contrary or exception to the general rule of the Scriptures is guidance for everyone. Yet, if some people have the wrong intention and attitude, they can harm their own selves.

Religious Attitude, and Behavior

The Real Achievement

One can ask God to give openings on the path of God through inviting people to religion and people's engagement with the Scriptures, the prophets, and Submission to God.

One can ask for these true openings for religious people and for non-religious people from God. One should ask that God is pleased with all of these openings, and that these are loyal servants and they are not poisonous honey on the path of God.

Yet, one should remember that all of the true openings on the path of God with which God is pleased, are still given by God. Therefore, one can and should ask God for these real and true openings. It is again from the Graciousness and Mercy of God that God is teaching us to ask for help from God- every day and constantly, initially, and regularly [26].

One of the conditions of these openings is establishing a prophetic atmosphere of gentleness. Yes, this critical atmosphere of the prophets is the key revival of God's message among religious people and non-religious people.

Gentleness: The Prophetic Atmosphere

One asks: What does gentleness means?

Gentleness is the prophets' atmosphere of

- ▶ acceptance,
- ▶ tolerance,
- ▶ overlooking faults,
- ▶ non-judgmental character,
- ▶ smiling,

- making ease and desiring easiness for people,
- comforting and solacing character,
- accepting everyone at their level with their gender, culture, and ethnic background
- when people make mistakes, forgiving them and asking forgiveness from God for them.

The above list can go further as the prophets' never-ending guidance for all creation. Yet, one should really understand some of the appealing character traits of the prophets are expressed and condensed with one word such as 'gentleness'.

Yet, this enablement of being gentle is given and bestowed on the prophets by God.

The prophets' atmosphere of gentleness can be a miracle. This miracle as the embodied character of the prophets can be similar to the miracles given to other prophets such as Jesus. Yet, all of the miracles can set guidelines and a goal for humans to achieve similarly to the prophets in order to please God.

From this perspective, one should constantly ask for this prophets' atmosphere and character of gentleness from God for achievements and openings in order to please God.

Peak of Gentleness

When we consider the above characters of the prophets expressed with gentleness, one should remember one of the utmost and peak parts of being gentle is that when people make mistakes, the person still forgives them and moreover, asks forgiveness from God for them.

Let us be honest and ask ourselves, "Who can do this?"

When we get angry, we lose ourselves. Then we start destroying ourselves and others.

When we get angry, if we try to control ourselves, we build up in ourselves this self-dialogue of hate, anger, and dislike towards people who made us angry.

When we get angry in this state, how many of us can relieve ourselves from this anger and can move on?

How many of us can move on, and on top of it, ask God to forgive them?

These are the prophets. This is the essence and core of embodying gentleness.

The Real Embarrassment

Embarrassment or modesty can be a state of the heart and mind that we are increasingly losing everyday in the current popular culture, especially with globalization via internet and media.

Modesty is becoming an increasingly lost term. Modesty with people, modesty with creation, and most importantly, modesty with God are all becoming theoretical concepts. Ultimately, modesty with God leads to etiquette and morals with God and accordingly, etiquette and morals with teachers, elders, parents, and others [27].

A person of modesty embedded in this culture can easily lose this valuable trait due to being considered as an outcast in this society. Especially, when teachings of modesty are frowned upon and actually, having no modesty or etiquette and morals is constantly presented and encouraged at all levels of education as part of the critical thinking and liberal approaches and freedom.

In these societies and times of absence of modesty and etiquette and morals, what should one do to not be hopeless or pessimistic?

Modesty requires minimizing the embarrassments or humiliation. The real humiliation occurs before God.

In this sense, the people who are in this real embarrassment are in front of God.

Therefore, it is important to ask God constantly not to have this real embarrassment and humiliation.

The Embodiment of Modesty

It is important to understand and analyze the notion of modesty.

In this regard, the Scriptures mention the embodiment of modesty. Having modesty from people is also a virtuous quality that one should have and maintain. Yet, the real modesty always should be with God.

For example, not exposing the faults of couples in marriage conflicts or problems is part of this modesty. Not exposing a person's faults to others is part of this modesty. Having modesty of not doing a permissible action can all be parts of this modesty depending on the level of the person.

Change and Religious Adaptation

This can also signify the need for the interpretation of the teachings according to time and place. In other words, the main teachings of the religion do not change. But, the people of God, the scholars need to bring the reviving principles of the religion depending on the spiritual diseases of the time, generations, and places. From this perspective, the teachings of the religions are not only the legal laws. If there are different influences due to various reasons from different places at different times throughout history, the scholars should present these teachings in a reviving format.

In this perspective, especially at our time, the Cognitive Behavioral Education with Therapy (CBET) similar to CBT (Cognitive Behavioral Therapy) from the religious practice can be important. In other words, the struggle concept now replaces itself with the logical, genuine, and practical discourses to persuade the people and to remove these diseases from the minds and hearts. One can call this CBET of the Scriptures and the Actions of the prophets. Some of the scholars used to call "Scriptures' Operatic System", OS with the Scriptures in people's minds. In other words, one of the contemporary scholars [28] used to ask this question: "How did the Scriptures make a huge change in the minds and hearts of the immediate followers, students or disciples of the Prophets? Why does this change not exist at our time? How can we contemporize this original motivation for our time?"

Victories and Openings after Being Patient

It is very difficult to not argue. Especially, when we live during a time when generating conflict is understood to be a virtue rather than a problem. Argumentation, confrontation, and questioning for the sake of questioning are the approaches of the modern society. Even, this attitude went in such an extreme, so out of control, that one can find books in popular media especially in the West titled as "Arguing with God".

This is the full loss of etiquette and morals. The people are so very disconnected from the notions of etiquette and morals but filled with the notions of arrogance embodying the 'I', 'me', or 'myself'. Unfortunately, in a globalized society with internet and others, religious people are deeply and greatly being affected by these diseases. Yet, by titles they can still be religious people, and God knows all of our essences.

In one of my ethnographic works with Yemeni communities, [29] one of the imams (priests) made a comment saying, "Today's religious people are worse than the pre-religious Arabs in morality and ethics." It was shocking for me to hear that from someone who is Arab and from Yemen where the genuine teachings are still practiced in nomadic or Bedouin society. Yet, he was alluding to the widespread notions of ethical problems such as bribery, cheating, lying, using the religion with politics and not hesitating to amplify the personal and social conflicts in lieu of personal gain in religious societies. Although I disagreed with him in that we cannot generalize this statement, yet one can question the essence of Submission today and how it is practiced and understood today compared to the time of the prophets and earlier ancestors.

Although critical thinking and questioning with etiquette and morals in order to understand and change one's position is a virtue, our point is the problem of the increasing trends in lifestyles promoting individualization in modern societies that break any type of bonds including family bonds, parent-child bonds, husband-wife bonds, and others. This is a social effect as an external agent shaping the individual with expected norms in the society.

Another perspective of difficulty arises intrinsically when the person holds the self or raw ego as the self-submission which does not like to follow, does not like to take orders, and does not like to submit but has the inclinations of opposition, confrontation, and shows the inclinations toward arrogance. This is the intrinsic perspective of an internal agent shaping the individual with its tendencies.

Both internally and externally, there are the effects of Satan amplifying this chaos and disunity among the individuals, families, friends, and in the societies.

With all of these different challenges, if the person still bears with patience and does not join the general club of 'people with problems', the person can have great openings of goodness to please God in his or her life. In other words, God can give a lot of enablement, blessings, and achievements to this person with the Divine Graciousness and Mercy.

The reason for these great openings is that it is very difficult to not be angry and to maintain patience with composure, and to not fight or argue in different relationships. These relationships can be between the husband and wife, children and parents, and in other relationships.

On the other hand, when we analyze the life of the prophets, their lives give examples of how one can achieve and overcome these difficulties.

One should recognize that the prophets are ordinary human beings, however, characteristically special, elected, elevated, and peaked in different parts of submission of God.

One of the charming features of the prophets is their being gentle- having a soft, gentle, empathetic, caring, pleasant, and loving character. During incidents when a normal or a pious person or a protectory of God had the possibility of losing control of himself or herself, the prophets still maintained gentleness, calmness, composure, and fully pleasant attributes.

On the other hand, one should remember that at the end of these self-struggles of cleansing the heart from the spiritual diseases of envy, and being patient, there may still be remnants of these diseases before one dies and failed outcomes of not being patient. With the Grace and Graciousness of God, God can remove them. This can be due to the constant and unending struggle of the person with oneself to embody patience and the character of gentleness similar to the prophets.

It is very critical to ask for patience and embodiment of the character of being gentleness from God as this character was also given to the prophets by God.

If God does not give it to the person, even if the person goes to the best psychologist or counselors in the world, the person will still be harsh and lose oneself in easy or difficult challenges of life.

Each stored potential energy in a person due to the unjust behaviors of others can have an opening for the person as mentioned in the sayings of the prophets that God is with the ones who are oppressed and who have broken hearts and their prayers and supplications are accepted as they are the oppressed [20].

Here, the struggle of the person towards the removal of these diseases is the key. Therefore, God can show the Divine Graciousness and Grace to remove them so that they can enter Heaven if there is the intention and struggle of removing these diseases.

One should first recognize and accept one's spiritual problems to move on to the next step of removal.

For example, one could invoke submission to God by truthfully saying: Oh God! Do not leave us with our own selves for even less than a second!

Oh God! We cannot do without You.

Oh God! Please make us have the character of gentleness similar to the prophets.

IMBIBING PATIENCE

Jasmin used to lose her temper. Each time she lost her temper she used to regret and blame herself about not being patient. She suffered pain after each incident of impatience. One day, she said to herself, "I don't know what to do." Then she started reading the scriptures and reviewed all of the verses about patience. After, she was once again convinced logically that she should not lose her temper. Then, she felt better and promised to herself that she would be more mindful in applying patience.

IN PRACTICE

To imbibe patience is very important. It is a continuous struggle to embody the true meaning of patience. One of the ways to implement patience is with prayer. Another way is constantly being mindful that seemingly evil occurrences can be a gain if one is patient. This notion is constantly advised in the scriptures. God is with the one who is patient. God is the supporter of the patient one. A person should always rely on God in the instances that require patience. Patience can be applied when facing evils. Patience can be applied for being on the right path. Patience can be applied for the struggles against one's own self if it encourages the person to do evil. If a person starts complaining and blames others, then at this stage there is no patience. This is the stage where the blame comes into the relationship with God. The relationship becomes shaky and unfruitful. Therefore, religious people practice chanting *'Praise be to God'* to appreciate God. In the instances where utmost patience is needed, they chant *'God is sufficient for me.'*

DISCUSSION QUESTIONS

1. Is it difficult to implement the notion of patience?
2. Why is patience a virtue in many spiritual and religious traditions?

The Path of God—Stability

One can be on the path of God with a positive change. In this positive change, there is always an energy and activism to do good work to please God. One calls this chivalry. The fuel of nondepleted energy to always do the righteous deeds, virtuous acts, can stem from chivalry regardless of one's age.

On another note, one should see this positive change as an asset. A person always looking for opportunities, changing the format, and adapting and updating oneself with the context to achieve goodness and yet at the same time being careful with the bad actions. This attitude can be boosting vertically and positively in one's relationship with God. In this regard, change is a good phenomenon. This is encouraged. One can also refer to this struggle as the struggle of adaptation, change, and still maintaining an increase in one's relationship with God.

In this perspective, positive change and the path of God are related. In other words, people can assume linearity or stagnancy or passivism on the path of God. Yet, the path of God can entail positive change while having incremental or linear increase in one's relationship with God.

In this perspective, the path of God does not entail passive adaptation of daily rituals. It is the effort of keeping one's daily rituals with constant embodiment of the meanings and recitations and yet at the same time, looking for more opportunities of positive change and increase in quality and quantity.

The expression and constant required repetition of the prayer in our supplication can indicate this dynamic and positive changing effort of the path of God compared to its negative or passive assumed interpretations.

In this case, one adapts constant positive change, means, or reasons in order to achieve and do good deeds. We should be constantly looking at the means or opportunities with a positive change to please God. This effort in itself as the real struggle can keep the person on the path of God of positive and linear increase in one's relationship with God.

The path of God, in this sense requires holding your initial asset and building on it. The path of God requires continuity of the positive change. The path of God requires predictability about this person's traits such as this person always runs behind the opportunities of doing the good deeds. The path of God indicates chivalry and positive change and upholding and invigorating spiritual enlightenment.

Societies, communities, business ventures, and families require the path of God. In this regard, the path of God requires stability, growth, trusted bonds, stable markets, and unified families. With the path of God societies, communities, business ventures, and families can grow positively and there can be a linear increase.

Then, one can ask: What is a negative change and how can it be related with hypocrisy?

Hypocrisy is the opposite of the path of God. Hypocrisy indicates negative change or negative energy for negative change. Hypocrisy indicates gloominess or darkness. Hypocrisy indicates unpredictability. Hypocrisy indicates not having set values, goals, and aims. Hypocrisy indicates change not for positive virtuous acts, but change built on self or lowly temporal interests or motivations. Therefore, when humanity regardless of religion, gender, ethnicity, and other differences, is happy all together about a virtuous act of achievement that benefits everyone, people of hypocrisy can be sad and crying for this unification of the common good. Hypocrisy indicates disunity and chaos in the humanity's shared ethical and moral values.

Chaos, instability, distrust, and volatility caused by hypocrisy can cause societies, communities, and families to decline in their spiritual and worldly growth. In the families where there is hypocrisy, the families cannot support each other with peace and tranquility. These families, sooner or later, are likely to break up and all of the family members become enemies to each other as if the parents did not take care of these children, as if the spouses did not spend many years together, and as if the children do not carry the same kinship bonds of being from the same mother and father. In these business markets of hypocrisy, businesses cannot grow, and they are always hesitant to make new investments.

Hypocrisy can fuel the desire for unfair exclusivity and privilege. The prime example of this unfair exclusivity or privilege was presented by Satan.

Exclusivity or privilege is not a right and is thereby given on merit. This is a statement in today's civilized society that has become a law. Having a driver's license in New York is a privilege but not a right according to the laws of New York State [14]. It is gained on the basis of merit. The person should embody the struggle, effort, and means to have this privilege.

Similarly, God chooses with the Divine Will Power however and whomever God wants. God is All Wise and All Knowing.

Although God does not need any explanation in the Divine Choice, Will Power, God still explains to us that God makes every decision with wisdom.

Yet, when God gives this honor of choice, then the person should make praise although the responsibility can be heavy.

God's Divine Will Power chooses individuals for a higher purpose by merit but yet with the Divine Graciousness . It is against etiquette and morals in regards to God to seek for a privilege personally similar to Satan.

Asking for privilege can indicate arrogance most of the time. A privilege given without asking can indicate uneasiness or discomfort in the individual due to its responsibility.

Hypocrisy can embody the desire to always have more than others in worldly means. Hypocrisy can desire more privilege than others in worldly means. Therefore, hypocrisy can require injustice and unfairness in order to satisfy the privileged groups.

Religion in the Lives of Individuals

Theodicy

Sometimes, evil-seeming incidents push our limits of understanding the wisdom and reason behind them.

Yet, even if the person knows the reasons, our human judgments call an evil-seeming incident as evil. Therefore, even if there is a relief by knowing the reasons, there may not be full relief.

In our human valuation system of assigning meanings, such as assigning something or someone as 'being in pain', suffering and happiness are due to our social and human constructions of meanings.

God knows everything beyond their time with their apparent and hidden manifestations in their true realities of purpose, value, and assignment.

With this comprehensive preface, surrounding, and inclusivity with power and knowledge, the creation purpose, goal, the existence in the world, the lives and the positions of all creation in this life, afterlife, and more, are all and fully known by God.

Our judgment calls and valuations, and assignment of meanings on things, events, or people all based on our knowledge. If we do not have the comprehensive knowledge of something, then there will be naturally and normally wrong and false deductions, interferences, and analysis.

Therefore, all evil-seeming incidents are not evil unless they are assigned and classified by God as evil.

Therefore, in a broader perspective, all the deductive reasonings can possibly be wrong unless they are checked with the inductive guidelines given by God through the teachings of the Scriptures and the prophets.

The absolute comprehensive knowledge is the true inductive guidelines, valuations, and assignments as set by God.

Humans' efforts are to try to approximate the true knowledge of inductive guidelines as set by the Scriptures and the prophets through the incremental steps and struggles of deductive reasonings in lifelong journeys.

For example, an evil-seeming incident can happen to someone. He or she may die or be killed due to oppression of people for this person's ethical and true stance on the path of God with his or her belief. Then, everyone around this person can interpret this with different explanations. Media or outside observers can amplify the effects of this evil-seeming incident. Then, people or the public start developing fear in their inner selves. Then, people may alienate from religion due to this evil-seeming incident as if the religion was not able to help this person and the religion was the cause of this. Then, they blame God in these evil-seeming incidents called 'theodicy' as a technical term.

Similarly, one can think about the case of slaughtering an animal for eating purposes. From the externality of vegetarians, it seems to be a very cruel act of killing something which has a life. Yet, we judge through our human observations which is normal. Yet, God is Just, The Utterly Just and The Most Merciful. God does not oppress anything or anyone, not even something smaller than a thin hair.

In the Scriptures, it is repetitively mentioned and emphasized in similar, different forms that God does not oppress.

We sometimes ask this question, "Is what happened fair?" Then, we question the fate given by God. Yet, everything happens with fairness and justice even though we may not realize and see it.

Nothing or no one is oppressed. Everything and everyone is treated with justice.

Yet humans precede their own valuation over God. Then, they blame God with evil, injustice, and other reasons of alienation as one can see in Western philosophy and religious thought.

THE LOST PHONE

One day, Hannah was packing for travel and could not find her phone. She checked her car. She checked her handbag. She could not find it. Although she could not imagine traveling without her cell phone and felt uneasy about it, she also thought about how nice travel could be without being bothered by the phone. She remembered that the only person who called her was her husband and he was already traveling with her. In the meantime, Hannah was also trying to understand the possible wisdom behind the evil-seeming incident of losing her phone. Using her husband's cell phone, she texted her own phone. "If you find this phone please text me." A day later, a person texted that she found her phone. After coming back from her trip, Hannah went and picked up the phone. The person who found the phone was an artist. Hannah gave her a nice gift to thank her for returning the phone. The artist had an interest in Hannah's themes reflected in her artwork. Then, Hannah now understood the wisdom of losing her phone: a possible long-term friendship between Hannah and the artist.

IN PRACTICE

It is important to interpret the evil-seeming incidents with a possible positive outcome graced from God. Sometimes, people's immediate negative response to evil-appearing incidents can ruin their entire life. The notions of patience, wisdom, and reflection should be practiced in all encounters of life.

Etiquette and Morals with God

One should remember that the whole purpose of religion is to instill the etiquette and morals with God. Etiquette and morals with God require one to have etiquette and morals with what God taught us to have etiquette and morals toward. Having etiquette and morals with the Scriptures, the prophets, and other parts of the etiquette and morals all stems from the core etiquette and morals with God. This core etiquette and morality with God stems from the oneness of God.

As the person increases true knowledge about God, then their etiquette and morals with God should increase. The effect of knowledge, aging instilling the person wisdom, or 'worship' are all expected to increase one's closeness and etiquette and morals with God. If not, then none of them have any use. If it is not helping the person to have more etiquette and morals with God than on a previous day, then the person is in loss. Accordingly, one can increase his or her etiquette and morals in the reflections of the primary etiquette and morals with the prophets and Other Beings of religion.

Aging or getting older is another means through experience in order to increase one's etiquette and morals with God. It is another means to increase respect for the Other Beings as God tells us to have these mannerisms with it.

In this sense, the realms and encounters of fate as the manifestation of the Divine Decree of God requires etiquette and morals with it as the required part of the etiquette and morals with God. In this sense, this etiquette and morality regarding fate and in its relation with God can be entitled as trust in God's plan, submission, and trust in general.

Trust in God's plan can mean 'I will come and listen to you'. Submission can mean 'I will do whatever you tell me with no question'. Trust in general can mean 'I am fully in submission to you'.

Even in the most difficult cases of evil-seeming incidents such as a bodily torture or at the time of death or during the pains of death, the person is still expected to keep this high standard of etiquette and morals with God. For example, when Abraham was about to be thrown in a hot oven and grill of fire, he did not complain a bit. Yet, his etiquette and morals with God manifested as only turning to God with full trust in God's plan, submission, and trust in general. Therefore, the title of Peaceful Heart, 'Friend of God', is given to Abraham by God.

When the person is afflicted with an evil, the etiquette and morals require them to admit the Power and Protection of God and turn to God for kindness.

This disposition as taught by the prophets reminds the person what their disposition should be with God, our Creator. We are all creations, servants of God. Then, asking kindness is critical.

In other words, we do not have to be in difficulty in order to prove ourselves to God.

When difficulty strikes we need to hold on to proper etiquette with God in order not say or do something that is displeasing to God. At the same time, asking constantly for easiness, kindness, and forgiveness as we are weak is important in all states of this difficulty. The person should always be in the state of asking easiness from God. We can lose at any time due to our weakness. Going back to God is critical.

Saying "I wish" is not having proper etiquette and morals with fate.

Death and Theodicy

It is interesting to note that God specifically mentions that death occurs not randomly but with permission and fate, destined by God.

Most of the time, the evil-seeming incidents are defined as evil because they seem to happen randomly. But this is not the case, especially with the random-looking cases of death. Everything, especially something critical like death, happens with the permission of God. God tells people to not worship and idolize the worldly reasons that causes a person's death.

Scriptures as a Blessed Inductive Guidance

It is also important to note that after the revelation of the Scriptures, the themes are directed to a focus on nature, science, earth, skies, and space.

Therefore, some of the scholars triangulate the learning from the revelation of the Scriptures with the knowledge from the sciences.

The message of the scriptures and the prophets is not new. God sent the same message and guidance since the time of the creation of Adam and the message with the Scriptures will remain until the Day of Judgment. In this regard, religion is not new, but a continuation of the previous messages. All of the Divine Books show the continuation of one to another. Therefore, there is a mention in each scripture for the upcoming next scripture. All of the messengers and prophets of God show the continuation of one to another. Therefore, there is a mention in the sayings of the prophets for the next prophet or messenger of God. Therefore, the proclamation of faith in religious creed necessitates that a believer is required to believe in all the Books and Prophets sent by God. If someone embraces only their own prophet or book and says, "I only believe my prophet or book," this can be other means of alluding against the Just Attribute of God.

In other words, thinking that God did not send a message, prophet, or guidance at other times to other people is a wrong construction about God implying that there was no divine guidance. God is Just, Merciful, and Caring. God does not leave people without guidance. But it is the person's choice to decide, to accept, and to follow. This establishes a true, robust, and genuine authenticity in rational and mindful methodology of religion.

During the process of delivery of the divine message to humans, there was no misinterpretation or a personal spiritual experience as this notion is common in Western engagements of religion.

In other words, we hear a lot of assertions from different religious groups, the statements of "I am inspired," or, "God inspired me." Although these personal inspirations can be relevant and genuine, but there is still the possibility of deception. So, God places another level of authenticity and assurance that the Scriptures are not a personal interpretation or experience. There is a process of delivery similar to other books or scriptures.

When you experience this with your own heart, then you would invite others as well. After one experience of the divine messages- in this case the revelation, the next stage of embodiment follows. One of the titles of the prophets was as the "Walking Scripture" [7]. This title shows the full embodiment of the scriptures in the life of the prophets. This embodiment is called actions of the prophets or the sayings of the prophets in tradition.

Therefore, the full human embodiment of the revelation, the Scriptures, is the life and practices of the prophets. This is called actions of the prophets or the sayings of the prophets. Therefore, the sayings of the prophets or actions of the prophets is as important as the Scriptures. The prophets demonstrated as humans in their lifespans the Divine Will through to the Scriptures. Some people may call this the application of the theory. But calling the Scriptures with this referral may not be correct and respectful in genuine religious discourses.

Translations of the Scriptures are not the Scriptures but interpretations. This phrase is repeated in various places in the Scriptures to emphasize and underline this notion. When any text is translated, then it is not the original text anymore but interpreted meanings of the text in that language. This means that there is room for error. The text should be understood in the original language within its context.

Another level of authenticity is that the Scriptures were mentioned in the previous scriptures sent by God and if you do not believe it, then you can review the scholarship in other books as also testified by their scholars. The scholars of other scriptures know it. Therefore, the Scriptures strongly criticize these scholars. They know it but they do not reveal it and inform about it.

God establishes repetitively the authenticity of the Scriptures by gauging the reader about the people's ungrounded thoughts and ideas opposing them with the same wording. Humans, Other Spirits, and Satan are given free choice and act accordingly but this free choice has also its limits. One of the places of their limit is that Satan, people, or Other Spirits do not have access and freedom to interfere with the true revelation of God.

God does not give the ability, means, and free choice to these beings in the realms of claiming the Scriptures were sent by anyone else except from God since it is the last Book of God. In other words, being the last scripture from God necessitates that it should remain the same until the End of Days. Therefore, these beings will not be given permission, willpower, nor ability to alter the Scriptures even though they may want to change it. Here is a place where the free will of humans, Other Spirits, and all of creation is blocked.

In another perspective, one should realize that it is a favor for every individual to realize that the Scriptures are a blessing for everyone. For each person, the Scriptures are a huge blessing in one's personal life. As the person can make praise and show gratitude and thankfulness to God for one's health, wealth, and welfare in one's life. One should also really show a similar or even more gratitude, thankfulness, and praise for the Scriptures from God. One can appreciate the Scriptures more if the person acquires the knowledge about the current situation of prior scriptures sent by God. In the scholarship of these scriptures, there is no similar discussion of authenticity compared to the established authenticity of the Scriptures. When a person is not comfortable reading a text, whether it is revealed by God or not, the person can easily be turned off before even starting to read about it. Therefore, it is not surprising to find other religious followers being turned off by their religion and changing and seeking for other religions that would have more authentic texts from God. The logic or intellect necessitates this disposition.

One of the reasons could be to remind the person that there is a reason for everything happening. In other words, the Western understanding of theodicy can alienate some people from God. Therefore, when a religious person reads scriptures, it is a reminder on a regular basis that there are meanings for the evil-seeming incidents happening constantly and that we don't understand their real meanings.

In the scriptures, there are examples of trials, tests, and the trait of patience is to be embodied with these incidents. The importance of youth is that most of the time the spirit of youth can handle challenges as compared to the people who are spiritually worn out. There are a lot of old aged people who are spiritually fresh and there are a lot of young people who are spiritually old. There are a lot of writings on the concept of chivalry.

God shows that if one is patient, then God gives that one victory. The above example is a case where it is first proved to the people themselves, as well as to the people around them, and then to the generations after and until the Day of Judgment as mentioned in the Scriptures.

But still the reality of the potential evil and jealousy of humans can be present. Therefore, caution and prudence are some of the means of making prayer and asking for protection from God.

The case of God's promise is mentioned that the patient ones will be the ones who will be in success and in victory with the promise of God. This is witnessed through the scripture's teachings about the past nations.

The central theme of patience comes as comparison here. It can be easier to implement patience when one is with the people of God who are constantly in worship. During the times of grief, it is important not to focus on the loss or the source of grief but on the discourses and relationship with the people of God. Do not even take your eyes from the people of God. Most of the time people agree that patience is a virtue, but they do not know how to practice it. Therefore, one of the practical suggestions is that when the person is with the ones who are close to God, then it will be easier and it will help the person to be patient.

When there is a problem, we tend to seek people's help. Then, most or all of the time the problem gets worse and we get into depressive states. Then, over time, as a blessing from God, we start forgetting the magnitude of the initial effects of this problem, as human means the 'one who forgets'. Then, the effect of this problem fades. On the other hand, if the person takes another route when the problem happens, that is, to run to God to solve, to beg, and to cry, then, the person can transform this evil-seeming incident into a very fruitful opportunity. One can really have an opportunity to use and make an advantage of this evil-seeming incident. Yet, there are very few who have this approach. Today's increasing number of mental clinics can be proof of this although they are needed for the ones who don't know how to transform these evil-seeming incidents into an opportunity for a mental and heart boost making the person self-dependent, confident, and strong with reliance on God. Rather, the person becomes dependent on the medicine, these clinics, and humans.

The real friend and protectory is always God. It is expected that the person should realize this at all times: at the end, during and before all trials, losses, gains, in good health and wealth.

Then, the case of these false attachments, position, wealth, and status are presented as the illusion or garbage of the world. It can be trashed at any time by God.

Other examples of attachments and problems are presented but then the good work always gets the points and rewards from God.

Also, in this chapter it is interesting to note that when people don't appreciate God and follow evil, and the chief of it, Satan, God reminds humans of this expected genuine relationship between the person and the Real Giver, God. How can one not appreciate God if this person does not recognize the Creator and follows the evils as represented and monumentalized with the word 'Satan'?

Now, the real case of patience and the unseen realities for the evil-seeming incidents reveal themselves. At times, an elect Prophet of God may not be able to fully rationalize these evil-seeming incidents. One can see the difficulty of the reality of patience in evil-seeming incidents as part of the test and trials.

This is another knowledge gained and given by God. This knowledge is given to an agent or messenger of God, who is not visible all the time but visible sometimes. This is internal knowledge given by God. The etiquette and morals of prohethood are seen in that when something evil happens, it is important to blame the Satan and the self.

One can review the existence of different types of sciences. This can show that even the great prophets of God do not know certain sciences. This can bring a perspective to accept everyone and that there can be some perspectives and knowledge that God gave to each person. What they are good at can be different and we can learn from them.

So, the question is not being jealous of what people know as knowledge. Or it is not position of "I know everything" but accepting that the person needs learning with humbleness and humility from others. In natural sciences, social sciences, or in spiritual sciences of heart and mind, one can always seek the knowledge with the position of learning even though he or she can be called an expert. If it is not someone's field of specialization, then it deserves more attention to learn from what the person does not know.

> The repeated key expression against evil is patience in the scriptures. Explicitly, it is repeated for the reason that it is not easy to be patient.

It is difficult to be patient because our human intellect requires reasoning and when we cannot, then this point is alluded.

One can find different depictions of evil seeming incidents in their true reality in the scriptures. In reality, they are not evil but mercy and grace from God, the One, Adonai or Allah.

As an example, the first case of evil can involve a group of good people ready to be oppressed by an oppressor and God can send a someone or something implicit or mystical to perform an evil-seeming incident to protect them from a bigger evil with a small evil-seeming incident. So, God is protecting, and it is important to be patient.

It is important to realize the etiquette and morals with God. The etiquette and morals with God require one to not render anything bad, evil, or unpleasant with God.

The second case of evil-seeming incidents is about the loss of our attachments such as things related with wealth, children, job, or position even though it can seem that we may not deserve to lose them. But God teaches that the inner reality that God gives the person is better than what he or she loses if the person is patient and still carries gratitude for God. Then, the person can still maintain a close relationship with God. At the end, the person can receive something better than what the person had before.

It is again important to realize the etiquette and morals with God. The life of someone is not a pleasant action. The etiquette and morals with God require one not to render anything unpleasant with God. Therefore, God creates the means for the death of people. Yet, everything happens with the Will Power of God.

The third case of evil-seeming incidents is that we feel so sad about a case because the person is helpless to help a child, or people in war, that we feel flooded with mercy so high that we think and question about the mercy of God. But God takes care of everything and plans as the Best Planner and as the Most Merciful. God gives the real ability and empowerment. One should remember that the person or agent is not the real implicit or explicit doer.

As this is the case of an orphan, there is an indication that God directly takes care of the needs of the orphans without any means. One can also remember the sayings of the prophets that the person who raises an orphan will be very close to the prophets.

The next set of cases can be performed by another agent or Prophet of God, but this time acting explicitly and this agent can have a position and strength to prevent evil in the society.

God is the One who gives the real ability or enablement to the person or agent. They are not the real implicit or explicit doers. They are just simple causes enabled by the Real Doer, the Cause of all causes.

The first case can be an evil done openly and publicly. God sends a prophet to establish justice and to remove evil and oppression.

The second case can be removing an evil related with life difficulties.

The third case can be about preventing the evil of people oppressing others.

The humans judge externally about these cases and they consider them as evil, but they do not know that an agent of God works to protect these weak people from evil and oppression.

In the second case, people are again weak, but they encounter a figure of justice, a powerful human like a prophet as the agent of God. The people in this case can see that the evil is prevented by someone and that they can externally judge that God sends someone to help them. One should note that the prophets in their language and communication with people constantly mention that they are the agents of God and acting with the help and empowerment of God.

In both cases, God helps humans and intervenes and prevents the evil. Now, the test or trial in all of these cases are the attitudes and perspectives of the person. Does the person blame God in the first case like we hear a lot? Or does the person say, "God sees me, watches me, and takes care of me." Unfortunately, we do not hear this perspective much but only a few times. So, this is the real test and trial. Believing and trusting in God in both cases of the visible and invisible seemingly evil incidents is the key.

The Cause of all Causes, God, has the authority over everything- allows, approves, or disapproves.

God knows everything. The questions directed by God are for us to learn and to reveal the true reality of the incidents that humans are not aware of because they are limited, and they act and judge with the apparent.

Prophets, Messengers, and Role Models as the Practical Source of Guidance

One can clearly see the prophets show the practical application of the Scriptures in their actions.

As the Scriptures set the main framework of teachings of religion, the prophets with the title of "walking Scriptures" show how this main framework is embodied and practiced in a religion's life. We should apply the teachings of the Scriptures in our lives as thought by the prophets.

The prophets indicate the notion of death in sleeping and waking up from death after sleeping.

Relationship with the Scripture and Prophets: Reminders

When the person forgets about God, then this can mean that the person does not read and apply teachings of the Scriptures and actions of the prophets. Therefore, the person does not know who he or she is without reading the Scriptures and actions of the prophets.

In that perspective, the Scriptures and the sayings of the prophets constantly explain who the person is in reality. The explanations of who created the person, what one's purpose and goal should be, what the nature, sky, mountain, animals mean, what death means, what evil and good means, what the seen and unseen realities are, what the limits of the person are, what the ethical and just ways in the relationship with the Creator are, with other humans, animals, and other beings. If the person does not know, does not learn and apply, then the person really can forget who he or she is.

In that perspective, God is Just. If the person makes the choice with his or her free will to disengage from these teachings of the Scriptures and actions of the prophets, then God can create the means and possibilities that this person wants in life. Then, this person can become the lost wanderer for his or her entire life. This person can think that he or she has a purpose, goal, and meaning but in reality, the person has wasted all of his life.

These people's situation in reality is so sad. They think that they are doing something good and logical. But in reality, unfortunately, they are wasting their time. The main reason is that when the message comes to them then, they are in the attitude of "I don't care." Or they make fun of and humiliate the people of genuine practice such as the messengers, or they make can make fun of the teachings of the prophets and the Scriptures.

Prayers, Alienation, and Theodicy

When a person makes prayer to God, then God responds to each person. In some cases, there is an immediate response. For others, there is the response if the person knows and understands it. In other words, God always but always answers, and corresponds to all sincere prayers of people.

In another perspective, since God answers all the prayers then, one should keep etiquette and morals with God while making prayer and asking from God.

If a person is given a high value by God, then when he or she calls God, then God immediately answers. In this case, the person should use this ability wisely with etiquette and morals and be thankful a lot for this blessing of God. In other words, God's answer and correspondence of all prayers in itself is a huge blessing and potential for a person. As the prophets mention, "Prayer is the weapon of a believer" [7].

PAIN IN THE EYE & THE PRAYER

One day, Adrian had a pain in his eye. He was thinking about what he should do. Then, he remembered the prayer of the Prophet about pains of the eye. He put his hand over his eye and read the prayer as suggested by the Prophet. The pain was immediately gone.

IN PRACTICE

It is important to follow all the teachings of the Prophet. If one applies these simple-looking but very effective teachings, then one can avoid a lot of different kinds of pain in life easily and quickly. In the above story, Adrian applied the Prophetic Teachings immediately instead of rushing to take a medicine from the pharmacy or calling a doctor.

DISCUSSION QUESTIONS

1. Do you ever use holistic medicines for common ailments?

Rituals as Collective and Social Engagements

Collective Rituals

Congregations of all believers and creation are asking and praying to God together. Also, when the person is praying, worshipping God, this is not possible unless there is the activation of the help of God. Therefore, the person can be praying to achieve the help and fortune of God. Therefore, in the sayings of the prophets [7] the prophets mention that when the person prays, God becomes this person's hand and feet figuratively as if God is helping this person due to this person's closeness to God with worship. As a result, this is given to this person by God.

Remove all the humiliating perspectives of reason which are reasons and means and then, directly ask from God about one's needs. The person does not consider any means or causes but believes and knows that God can do anything beyond the natural laws.

Company of Religious, Ethical, and Good People

Seek means to get close to God and to please God. The best means to get closer to someone is to be in the company of ones that this person loves. Similarly, the best way to please God is to be with the ones that God loves. The highest means are the prophets, in this regard, when the person follows the teachings of the prophets, the actions of the prophets. The title of the prophets are the 'Loved Ones', by God. When the person imitates the role models, the prophets, the genuine and practical learning will happen, which is pleasing to God.

Rituals in Representation of Divine Authority

Difference between All praise be to God and Glory be to my Lord Almighty

- ▶ All praise be to God is the divine phrase that signifies one's starting and beginning genuine relationship with God. In practice, anyone can use this phrase to establish relationship with God. Or, it could be in the language that someone can use it with an exclamation mark that the person may not fully internalize the meaning just as a sound of astonishment similar to "oh my God". At this level, this is still valuable and important and appreciated by God.
- ▶ Once the person goes beyond the first stage to the second stage of prayer, with full intention, reading the chapters from the Scriptures, this person is assumed to already be on the journey of establishing relationship with God. In this perspective, God lets from the Divine Graciousness and Mercy, the God attribute. Then, the expression 'All praise be to God' transforms at a personal embodiment level and becomes the rope as the connection point from general to specific as 'Glory be to my Lord Almighty the Protector' at the prostration. The person should know that the person already entered into the house and he or she is not saying 'All praise be to God', but 'Glory be to my Lord Almighty the Protector'. At this state and position, the person should maintain the highest caution and etiquette and morals of presence with God with perfection, the perfect union, being in the presence of God. For example, before the person

starts praying, he or she can be considered outside the house. As soon as this person starts praying, he or she is not outside anymore but inside the house now by being in the prayer. In other words, the person is in the Divine Presence now with God and talking to God.

▶ Once the person leaves the house, as an outsider as if saying goodbye, the person says 'All praise be to God' as a way of greeting and leaving the house.

Rituals as a Source of Solidarity

Religion and Globalization

Global Issues and Unification

One of the signs of this unification can be realized on global and common issues that we face as a humanity.

At another perspective of belief, God allows the display of different global issues such as a novel virus spreading throughout the entire world which ends up forcing a global action to take place. Or, consider the issues related with injustice, abuse, discrimination, or killings. This unified stance may also be referred to as universal realities affecting all of us that can remind us of the notion of unification with our values as the community of humans.

This one unification as community requires us to present our needs as one single body or unit to the One, God Who upholds and maintains everything.

This is one of the wisdoms of prayer in congregation as a unit. Realization of this presentation is one of the essences compared to our individual presentations to God.

In other words, realization of our God as a unit of all humans and presenting our needs can change anything.

One can remember the practice of the prophets [20] at the times of global need such as drought taking children, adults, and even animals and presenting our attitude as one in front of the One, God.

We can also realize this unified stance among religious people when there is a common problem such as religious phobia among people towards all religious people. At these times, regardless of the group identification, religious people tend to be together for this common problem among themselves.

Therefore, our attitudes should be always promoting commonality and not the conflicts.

Let the people realize the conflicts on the paths of interactions of commonalities!

If they want to make a meaningful change in their lives, be respectful to these changes!

God is the One Who is the Final and Ultimate Decision Maker and Judge.

God puts into perspective who the real community and the Creator is. Then, this true community, in their essence and core are the prophets, role models, and real leaders representing the pure, true, and genuine agents to follow. Once the person establishes this perspective, one can establish the oneness of God and the reliance. Most of the people accept God in Oneness of God, supplication, and sustenance. But then, they worship and practice wrong and not genuine things. In reality, this should also follow along with the true worship and practice in religion.

The Scriptures address different problems of belief as some have issues with supplication and some with sustenance and some with reliance. In its true sense as the prophets mention, a religion can still have remnants of these three problems internally or implicitly but not externally or explicitly as in the case of showing off mentioned by the prophets similar to a black ant walking in the dark [7]. This can be an implicit associating other with God. It may be very difficult to detect it.

Oneness of God has sustenance, supplication, and reliance. In other words, one must first establish the true oneness of God in sustenance to know who takes care of everything in the universe. Then, this should be the reason why one should have the true oneness of God with reliance and worship only God. Oneness of God in supplication necessitates recognizing explicitly one Creator as a creed. In all cases, one recognizes the Oneness of God in the creed of belief as the oneness of God in supplication, the Oneness of God as the care taker of everything in the universe as the oneness of God in sustenance, and reflecting this Oneness of God in the worship and worshipping only God alone and nothing else as the oneness of God in reliance. When this is all accomplished, then the sincere belief without any partners to God can be embodied in oneself.

Again, after one knows the true oneness of God in supplication, then this should immediately lead to oneness of God in reliance, that the person should worship only God. The highest form of worship is the supplication for showing oneness of God in reliance. The reason, outcome, and the fruit of all reliance is reminding oneself of God. In other words, reminding oneself of God is being always in the presence of God. The true reminding oneself of God is perfection at all the times in one's life.

These teachings are not something new. God sent at different times the same message with different messengers that the Creator is One and everyone should recognize this truly and worship God purely and solely.

God in the Scriptures gives different avenues, paths and approaches in one's personal spiritual journey so that the person can grab one and say, "I believe in and appreciate God." After going through all different possibilities explaining to us, God instructs the prophets to say that finally: "I am being instructed that Your Creator is One." After this are you going to believe?

"Are you not going to follow? Are you not going to be appreciative? Are you not going to leave the evil and your bad habits?"

The Prophets as the Unifiers and Minimizing the Conflicts

When one analyzes the character of the prophets for their entire lives, they have embodied the positive attitude of unifying people, minimizing conflicts, and making life easy on people. This is a manifestation of the trait of intelligence that one can be given as an intelligence with the Grace and Graciousness of God such as in the case of the prophets. Or, it can be an effort trained and gained opening to the blessings that increases one's spiritual level vertically.

All the actions of the prophets and the sayings of the prophets are really based on this principle of unification with oneness of God and also, unifying people and minimizing conflicts and making an easy and livable life for people.

In this regard, the prophets have the highest level among all humans. This is the essence of our human disposition as a social being.

There are thousands of examples of this stance in the Scriptures approving and showing this high status of the prophets as well as witnessed by the followers in the life of the prophets. This is not really an exaggeration but a reality.

Prophet Muhammed's problem solving and removing the conflict interference of black stone placement before prophethood [30], his preference of silence in response to the questions with the concern of responsibility of requirement, his patient disposition when his wife Aisha was slandered and when people were promoting conflicts, his easy choice about freeing the war captives, his exposure to rude and aggressive treatment and other personal encounters, and his maintenance of composure and serenity without getting angry although he had more power than the most powerful king in the history of the earth. Natural disposition of entertaining the kids compared to our current problematic understanding of etiquette and morals treating children with harshness, his kind treatment of the women although challenged by the women as compared to our problematic understanding of authority, his kind and tolerant disposition of people's social needs such as entertainment, food, and private life, recognizing our humanity and giving respite, his response to animal abuse, his response to and interaction with a crying tree, and there are many other examples.

One can review the life of Jesus in problem solving and his peaceful teaching to keep the calmness, serenity and peace [31]

One can review the life of Aaron and Moses in conflict resolution in the search of the Ideal Jewish peacemaker as mentioned [32]:

> "Some of the most important constructs of conflict resolution in numerous rabbinic sources are expressed by midrashic metaphor. The rabbis make the biblical figure Aaron, the high priest and brother of Moses, into the paradigmatic peacemaker."

One should understand that the prophets were humans and social beings, and yet at the same time, they were in the valleys and witnessed and embodied all of the dispositions of people in Hell, in the afterlife and in realities beyond our human world means. They have the closest experience with God as a social being and as a human as the Purest of all creation including the angels.

When angels met the prophets, they were honored for this blessed meeting that they had been awaiting for a long time. Yet, the same prophets came back as the humble and purest among us to be with us.

Therefore, the prophets will be the only ones in permission of interaction with God on the Day of Judgment as the ones who truly are embodied at the highest level, being Servants of God.

Global and Collective Challenges: Apocalyptic Approaches

One can ask this question about the possible wisdom regarding the of End of Times: Why or what can be the possible reasons that global challenges would increase as forecasted by the prophets?

When the people and individuals increase in their inner dispositions of, "We can challenge anything. We do not need any religion, God, or anyone. We have science to solve our problems," then one should consider if this is the voice of the majority or of the minority.

In other words, there can be individuals in this stance as a minority. Yet, when this way of thinking becomes the norm for the majority through secularized and required education systems, then a child in his or her pure mind can be brainwashed through modern means eight hours a day through a social level of policy making, and generations are raised with this mindset of absence of God in their lives.

In this system, religion, religious institutions, or parents cannot serve as mechanics trying to constantly make repairs and inserting or reminding them about God.

In other words, science, education, and all disciplines have a value in their details of scientific laws. Yet, these narratives make all of this education cold, purposeless, meaningless, random, and chaotic. On the other hand, mentioning the Name of God as the Real Doer makes the person and education system recognize these rules, laws, and scientific findings in their objective realities of being amazing means for the laws of God. Realizing and appreciating the Real Doer of the science makes the idea of knowledge an organic whole with interconnected micro and macro systems. There is a complementary meaning in recognizing these rules, laws, and science as the laws of God and creation of God.

The opposite approach or absence of God in learning and instruction cultivates individuals with arrogance, and pseudo or false confidence as constantly pumped up and sanctified by secular psychologists.

Then, these individuals at one point in their lives have a mental and spiritual crash to show them the opposite in its full reality. This full reality is that the person is weak and not independent. The person is fully and only dependent on God in every second. These means can be through personal witnessing of diseases or other difficulties.

Now, when this stance of absence of God becomes the norm globally, the reminders come as a form of global crash or a global humility, to show all humans otherwise- that all humans are weak and not independent, but fully dependent on God in every second.

When these trends become the norm, the global trends of crashes such as disasters can increase to remind the person and all of humanity as mentioned by the prophets.

These peak times can be referred to as 'antichrist' era. In this regard, 'antichrist' is nothing more than the symbol of representation of the majority of the people or humanity.

In other words, antichrist does not come out of nowhere in an unprepared society with unprepared norms. The prophets mention that the leader of the people is from the people [13]. In other words, if the people change, then the quality of leader changes. There is no point in criticizing the leadership if the people are representations of the traits of this leader. The leader is chosen from the people.

Similarly, Antichrist and other evil anti-religious people are only symbols of representations of the focused or condensed disposition of the people as a majority. They are the symbols of arrogance, and pseudo or false confidence of independence leading to their explicit claims as deities.

If our systems prepare the individuals with these false traits, then lead them to crashes in their lives, I think it is important to realize and objectively consider our positions.

Therefore, one can remember another of the sayings of the prophets which is that the End of Days will not come until the absence and disappearance of the people of belief on the earth [7]. In other words, as a Mercy and Graciousness of God, God does not terminate this system which is based on purpose, goal, and structure, as long as a single individual of choice or free will still exists and recognizes this goal and purpose.

When there is the absence of belief, then there is no reason or point of existence for the earth, stars, or galaxies for the people who see everything as chaos with their arrogant dispositions of pseudo and fake confidence.

Therefore, if the people of world, environmentalists, and others want this world to continue and not end, they need to recognize God at the same time. Yet, there is the fate of everything as set by God.

Apocalyptic Unification and Conflicts

It is interesting to see that there are specifically two names mentioned: Jesus and David. Jesus is the person that Christians expect the most benefit from in terms of their religious affiliation. Yet, Jesus curses them who associate others with God as disbelief in God for their less than genuine and altered religious dispositions. In the case of David, there is the expectation of Jews that the messiah would be from the descendants of David and there are a lot of renderings and preparation for it among them. In both cases, the person or people expect the most benefit from the benefactors ,but they themselves turn away from them. This should be very devastating and disappointing.

It is interesting to reflect on the wisdom of why this case is mentioned other than the immediate reasons at the time of the prophets. In other words, what are the implications of these verses until the End of Days? As the Scriptures do not have only meanings based on reason, but as they bear meanings for all times, where are their meanings today and in the future?

One possibility can be that the country or societies of Rum at the time can reflect today's Europeans or Westerns, or the Christian majority population. In this perspective, one can reflect that under rule of Westerns or Europeans with a majority of Christian population, believers maintain their religion in peace.

In other words, establishing justice or structure as a power representation should not be the main goal of believers in life. Yet, it is important to serve and work for justice and peace. Yet, there is an order and priority with everything. When religious people were facing all of the full injustice treatment, the prophets encouraged people to migrate to the societies where justice and peace had been established [33]. Yet, they mostly focused on relationship with God through the embodiment of the reality of the Oneness of God and accountability in front of God. One can talk about justice and peace if the person does not have a reference point of accountability and belief in God—in its absolute sense.. Oneness of God requires justice and peace in all cases of hidden and public engagements because the person believes in God and God is All Seeing.

In other words, if the establishment of justice is implemented by whomever God wills, that is important to accept.

What is important is to establish a proper genuine relationship with God and the rest can then follow. This also can be seen in the lives of Prophets and Messengers such as Abraham, Moses, Jesus, and Muhammed.

One should remember that emphasizing the commonality in our fate and religious traditions through the Oneness of God, referrals of deity with different names such as God, the One, Adonai, or Allah can help to establish an established order or a structure in a society. When we review the phrase as "in God We Trust" in American currency of dollars, there is a benefit of unification of unity represented by religion under complex system of immigrants.

When one reviews the sayings of the prophets during the End of Days as apocalyptic teachings about killing and mischief on the earth, the prophets mention that there would be turmoil in spite of the enormous population of religious people. This can again be due to misplacing the desire to establish a structured society with power over the real concerns of belief or oneness of God.

On another note, one can ask: Why are most of the prophets who are mentioned in the Scriptures in the area of the East or Middle East? Even, the Western dominant Christianity has its roots in the Middle East with Jesus. One can approach this question in many ways. One way can be from cultural perspective. The Eastern cultures have intrinsic qualities that dictate respect with the teachers, parents, elders, and other wisdom-based notions in their cultures. When one analyzes the Western societies of today, mostly mind and intellect-based approaches are dominant. Both are good qualities. Yet, belief requires humbleness, humility, and submission with respect. Mind is very critical, but it is not the first required element. However, it is complementary in religious sciences.

The events that we encounter in daily life in the world also have other dimensions, meanings, and purposes than how we see and interpret. In this perspective, the creation that we see in our daily lives such as trees, stones, sky, clouds, sun, moon, hot, cold, and all of the animals and others can have some other meanings. As mentioned, looking at everything with their connection to God, and with their connections to the afterlife, can have other meanings compared to how we interpret in their immediate literal meanings.

SIGNS & THE EARTHQUAKE

It was early Thursday morning and Kimber was reading her daily scripture in the temple. She kept falling asleep while reading a page where there were some punishments mentioned about the ungrateful ones. She woke up and tried to read the same page again. She again fell asleep while reading the same page. This happened a few times. There was a heavy rain with darkness outside. Kimber woke up one more time, glanced outside the window and said to herself, "Something is going on. May God protect us all." Shortly thereafter, Kimber got a text message from her husband about news of a major earthquake in the city where her parents live.

IN PRACTICE

Everything is a sign from God in life. God does not give life without any purpose and goal. Each second or minute of a person's life has a meaning and a purpose. No occurrence in life is by chance or by luck. Everything has a meaning if the person understands. If the person does not understand, anything big or small does not make any difference for this person due to that person's heedlessness or 'I don't care' attitude.

Layered Authority: Checks and Balances between Governments and Religion

When there is a group of people who may tend to do work together, the group leader tends often in public formal or informal venues to be asserted as a person working for others or spying. Identifying the leaders from this perspective looks like a common phenomenon that happened before and is happening today. From another perspective at a reflective point of the social incidents, if a person or group is accusing others to be spying there is always the possibility of this action being performed by this group or individuals. The concept of positive monitoring for public interest is a possibility. In this sense, negative or destructive spying is discouraged but positive monitoring for everyone's interest with justice without oppression is a possible practice.

There is an emphasis to allude to the intention of why people are engaged in a social or public discourse. Although what they support may not make sense, they do not want to be with the losers. As if they are saying, "We don't care who is right or loses, but we want to be with the winners".

When they were ordered to get together as an audience to observe the challenge between Moses and Pharaoh with his aristocrats, one can see the position of magicians making exactly the above statement as mentioned in the Scripture. They also want to be winners and get some benefit as an outcome from Pharaoh.

In this case, we can review three groups: the higher class, and administration, then, the magicians and then, the people. Both magicians and people who are the majority are motivated to fulfill the order because of their desire to be on the winning side and get something out of this opportunity. This shows that it is easy to manipulate the crowds especially when there is the representation of power and people and the general public do not want to be losers.

There is an expected attitude of submission and surrender with humbleness when there is an order or miracle from God. As mentioned in the scriptures, Magicians immediately embody their true position of being servants of God and they bow to God.

A similar case presents itself in the case of angels.

The understanding or going behind the reasons should come after, not before, for the true attitude of a person with etiquette and morals towards God. This etiquette and morality can be called a fear of God. Conversely in the case of Satan, he immediately uses reason instead of the etiquette and morals of submission and surrender.

It seems that it is the level of belief confirmed in the heart. Especially, this confirmation comes with difficulties and tests. With the context of magicians who are put in a trial and threatened by death by the Pharaoh, yet they still confirmed and held on to their belief. Therefore, they make the statement, "We hope that God forgives us because of us becoming the first believers."

The Prophet Abraham makes prayer to be remembered well in the later generations and to be from the ones that God is pleased with. God accepts his prayer and we in every supplication recite his name, also outside the supplication making prayer, and we read his name constantly in the Scriptures and in the sayings of the prophets.

In this case, who will remember the person- the angels or the people? God knows everything as we do not use the word 'to remember' for God. So, it is important to ask the best way of remembrance. If some people do not have good remembrance as mentioned in the Scriptures with curse, then this may be the opposite of this case, similar to Satan.

There are other people whom when they leave a place, job, town, or when they die, they want to leave a good memory or remembrance. A person leaving a job with a good remembrance may want to go back to that job again. A person leaving a town with good memory or remembrance may want to visit that town again. A person with good memory or remembrance by angels will want to meet with angels. A person whom God is pleased with will definitely want to meet with God.

There are very interesting points for the methods of outreach, characters of the prophets and messengers, the expected attitude or the reasons of loss, and the reasons of rejection.

Moses and Abraham were both in in an open method of making worship. Their methods and possibly characters were very fearless and they challenged the authorities openly without any self-consequence. Therefore, the lives of both Moses and Abraham were very much action-based. They changed their life conditions. They participated in migration and looked for more opportunities in different contexts, places, and times with different people and circumstances to invite them to God. These actions were either related with worship or learning knowledge. One can look at Moses's life in different places with his people learning the knowledge.

Similarly, Abraham changed his living conditions and challenged his own people where his father lived. Then, he moved to another place and challenged another king without any fear. Besides, Abraham inquired to learn from God about how God creates, and the case of creation of the birds with the witness of Abraham is mentioned in the Scriptures in this context. In this case of learning and knowledge, God taught Abraham directly as the 'Peaceful Heart', the Friend of God.

There are different levels of the prophets. In this perspective, Prophet Muhammad has the title of the one who is Loved by God. The Prophet Muhammad spent his entire life as a demonstration about the essence of these qualities of love, gentleness and caring. Jesus has the title of "the soul" of God. His soul did not have any means with a father similar to Adam. God removed the means of father as a miracle to authenticate their positions as a messenger from God. Moses has the title of the one who conversed with God. Abraham has the title of friend of God. All are very high titles.

Comparatively, one can review the lives of other prophets. Their softness and gentleness with their people were notable. They did not move or migrate to any other location but dedicated all of their lives to their people.

Abrahamic Religions and Special Commonalities

The first example is Prophet Moses representing the Jews, the second example is Jesus representing the Christians, and the third example is Prophet Muhammad representing the Muslims.

These are some themes in the Scriptures that come also to show that God sent at different times the same message. In this perspective, religious people are not only at the technical terms but they try to be the real and genuine followers of God by implementing the ethical and moral values.

God sends the prophets to teach the people. In this case, the prophets are the ones who are natural, pure, and genuine. Knowledge is important as long as it is genuine, natural, and pure and the person applies it.

The prophets mention the importance of useful knowledge in their prayer and that one should learn and increase knowledge in order to practice and act on it [34].

In this case, learning or acquiring knowledge is not an intellectual entertainment but it is a need to excel in one's relationship with God and to please God.

Being Religious and Spiritual

Negligence

When our life is long, when our engagements become routine, when we tend to ignore things, and this negligence becomes normalized, then this can form deep layers of negligence.

Fear or warning is a means to break the negligence, heedlessness [34]. The teeny and miniscule amount of trial or punishment that the person undergoes is a means to break the heedlessness but not really to punish the person, as indicated in the Scriptures.

In this sense, people may tend to ignore and do not give attention to something if they have some alternatives. In other words, we tend to prioritize our time, engagements, and preferences due to our limited time and focus. In this sense, we may deem something to be more important than something else.

If this is the case, whatever those implicit or explicit cases are, we cannot even help our own selves. We are ourselves in need.

Another point is that people expect identity, group, or clique-related ownership. People can have a strong social network and then there is an expected protection by an individual through this association. If this is the reason of preference, then this option is not possible in the case of one's relation with God. Then, this cannot also be a real disposition.

There are and can be people who are motivated with these false choices of preferences.

ONE HAND, ONE LEG, ONE EYE

Gwen used to practice having one hand, one leg, or one eye for part of each month. She would put one of her hands in a cast for a week and use only one of her hands. The next month, she used crutches to walk and to do her work and daily needs using only one leg. The following month she put a cover over one of her eyes in order to only use only one of her eyes for her daily needs and at work. Gwen did not tell anyone this secret. She was pretending as if an accident or something happened to her. Except one day, a friend deduced Gwen's secret practice, and asked for her reason. Gwen said, "I will tell you the reason only because you probably think I am crazy. I want to appreciate what God gave me. Sometimes, I see people around and they do not appreciate what God gives them and God tests them with difficulties. I want to truly feel this appreciation for God before any trial or evil hits me. You may still think that I am crazy, but it doesn't matter."

IN PRACTICE

It is really important to be in constant appreciation and in constant gratitude for the favors of God. Most of the time, people value what they lose. People are envious of what they do not have. In the above story, Gwen was trying to instruct and train her own ego for this true sense of appreciation of God.

DISCUSSION QUESTION

1. Why do people tend to look at others and notice what the others have but they don't have?

The Core of Negligence as the Monotonous Routines of Normalization versus Freshness of Surrender

The core reason of negligence can be indicated by the negation of other possibilities.

Our normalization of blessings can be a poison for us. When blessing are taken for granted, it can become like a poison. Then, these normalizations lead to the next step of unawareness, assumptions of blessings being normal and adopting passivism as a way of life. Spiritual passivism is spiritual inertia. The person does not want to change and be excited to the higher levels through the constant dispositions of awareness and amazements of faith. Yet, this spiritual inertia leads to spiritual laziness, heedlessness, and negligence. This hardening happens at the spiritual level of heart. These spiritual soft and liquid states of heart and soul change phases into a solid state over the course of time.

From the perspective of 'against', the opposite of the meanings…

In this sense, if the negligence happens immediately, then this can indicate the quick changing of character through breaking promises and lies. This unsettled character type with constant change, lies, and breaking of promises can indicate hypocrisy. Hypocrisy can induce the fury of the prophets and can lead to the fury of God. From another perspective, fury of the prophets against their people can induce fury of God on them.

On the other hand, if the negligence happens over extended periods of time, then this can lead to indication.

Spiritual Passivism and Activism

One of the side results of heedlessness is spiritual passivism. Spiritual passivism is the disposition of not acting when there is truth to be followed.

The sign of spiritual passivism is being heedless, and having an unchanging heart in the dispositions of remembrance of God.

Spiritual passivism is the disposition of not acting to change an evil. Spiritual passivism is the disposition of 'I don't care about others as long as I am okay'.

Yet, spiritual passivism leads to spiritual death. It can kill the person's faith to the point of no return.

The opposite of spiritual passivism is spiritual activism. Spiritual activism is the disposition of acceptance, open-mindedness, and following when there is truth to be followed. The sign of spiritual activism is crying and changing of the spirituality and heart.

Spiritual activism is the disposition of acting to change an evil. Spiritual activism is the disposition of constant concern about others, all living beings and things.

Spiritual activism or passivism is not related with age. There can be people who are 25 years old and they could be spiritually dead and passive. There can be people who are 85 years old who are spiritually fresh and active.

In this sense, spiritual activism is the 'young-manliness'. Young-manliness is the spirit of embodiment of remembrance of the One. Remembrance of the One leads to full reliance on God. Young-manliness is the spiritual activism that takes its full power from God. The worldly means of power, fear, or pain can all be minute or trivial as long as the full power comes from God through a prayer and remembrance of the One.

Middle Way

This word can imply a path of a highway that once the person enters it, then it is very difficult to leave. Also, here, the question of what is truth and what is falsehood is present. In this perspective, the middle way (or the straight path), instead of from one extreme to another extreme such as either having extreme hedonism or extravagance or extreme passivity, but the middle ground or middle way is always preferred.

Ability	Extreme1 Passivity	Extreme 2 Extravagance	Middle Way (Middle Ground)
Desires	Having no desire for anything	Having extreme desire, going over limits	Balance: Knowing the limits of permissible and impermissible for good, and ethical (Ex: allowed actions and prohibited actions)
Anger	No Anger	Extreme anger leading to oppression	Courage: Anger for Justice and for ethical
Mind	Using no logic	Using logic to mix the truth and falsehood such as demagogy or some political discourses	Wisdom: Using logic with wisdom for good and ethical action
Belief	No Belief: Not recognizing the self as a created being and not recognizing and appreciating the Creator	Mixing the Creator and created. For example: figurative language in scriptures	Unity, Oneness, Uniqueness of the Creator from the created.

Middle Way, Examples of the Straight Path

Gratitude

As the person is in the state of thankfulness even in the difficult situations, then God promises to increase what is already given. The constant state of thankfulness and praise can be achieved by pondering what one already has. This can imbue a feeling of constant thankfulness.

One of the traits that make the prophets people who embody this gratefulness and thankfulness is that they never complain when we normally complain in our lives. An unpleasant food, environment, or people are some examples of this when even those whom we consider to be good people can complain. Or, if we take it further, for example, hunger is one of the cases that causes people to lose their real self and become ungrateful, mean, and angry. The prophets did not complain but maintained most of their lives with hunger without complaining, but still being grateful and in thankfulness to God.

As one can realize the skies and the earth are big blessings, and bounty from God. For how many years, humans have been trying to find in outer space a similar system like earth and our atmosphere, but there is no sign of existence similar or comparable to ours. This simply can show that the earth and skies are big blessings for humans as their habitat. Therefore we must be thankful.

Spirituality: Focusing on the Heart, Emotions, Experience, and the Self

One can see that the gist of everything happens at the level of heart. God can change the state of one's heart depending on one's acquisition, acquirement, choice, execution of free will, and attitude.

For the person, it is important to detach the heart from everything but God. Therefore, in the field of mysticism, there are a lot of systematic methodologies developed to implement this notion of detachment and cleaning. For example, constantly taking care of it means, continuously looking at, and monitoring one's own heart spiritually.

So, the term 'healthy mind' refers to a state of heart detached from all of the ill and diseased feelings, but is only filled with the pleasure of God [35].

As the person looks at something or hears something, immediately feelings are formed in one's heart. In life it is very difficult to first diagnose and then to filter one's feelings and emotions. These could be positive or negative feelings. Negative ones could be the diseased feelings of superiority, arrogance, judgment, ungratefulness, etc. So, one can engage with reminders to remove the effect of these negative feelings. Yet, if the reminder is not internalized, the effect of the reminder can be limited in fulfilling the level of the healthy mind. From this perspective, the scholars of the internal sciences developed the practice of minimal talk, sleep, and eating so that one can increase in care and be as much as possible in constant monitoring of the heart. When all of those three- sleeping, talking and eating- are done in excess, they decrease the moments of taking care of the heart.

In other words, one should be monitoring their heart and thoughts always and this is called 'inner beautification'. The person does this to be aware that God is constantly watching the person and to detach themselves from everything except God.

In this state, the person naturally smiles because the person is in the true state of peace, happiness, and salvation. The smiling, gentle, kind treatment becomes the natural constitution of the person.

One can also review the sealing of the heart for hypocrites and other cases why and when it happens. If the person fills the heart with everything except God, then this heart dies, and it is sealed. The expectation for humans' spiritual journey is the opposite: emptying the heart from everything except God.

Emptying the heart can mean removing all of the crude and detailed ill feelings. Then, when the heart is empty, at this point, putting God fully inside becomes possible. In all of this process of emptying, discharging, and charging, God helps the person.

This state of the heart makes the person happy on this earth and in the afterlife or stressed, miserable, and fearful.

Conversion

The Real and Pseudo Self

Our real and pseudo self displays itself at different types of engagements. This can be social, kindship, or professional engagements. These engagements can be temporary in their nature. It may be difficult to display and control one's real identity or real-self in these engagements due to different social dynamics. For example, a person may do something because they may not want to upset someone or others, etc. It may be difficult to reveal one's own self, the inclinations, or the desires in a group engagement.

The real tendencies, desires, emotions and inclinations reveal themselves and the person can be in a self-dialogue mode. This is a permanent state as compared to the first case which is a temporary state. In the temporary state, there may not be the real self but rather a partial or opposite of the real self. Therefore, faith or negativity is in the second case when the real self is revealed with self-dialogue.

Therefore, the first state is a temporary state of sins or mistakes. A true believer can make mistakes and sins in different engagements. As long as when they are in the state of self-dialogue, self-accountability with repentance and regret, then God can forgive this person because his real self does not approve of this unreal self's mistake in different engagements. Therefore, the prophets mention that when a believer commits a sin, faith is not with that person at that moment. This can be called a pseudo or unreal or temporary self. All of the cases of sins instilled with fury, wrong judgment, or instantaneous change of the real-self can be an example of this pseudo self. The moments of, "What did I do? Why did I get angry? Why did I say this? I was not right, etc." as the cases of self-dialogue can show the disposition of the real self. This can be called in religious terms as seeking forgiveness from the One, regret, repentance, or seeking forgiveness from the One when this real-self verbalizes and embodies to the next step of asking forgiveness for this person's pseudo self's actions.

For whatever reason, there was this evil act, but this person was bothered by this. One can also analyze the cases of the pseudo self in the cases of anger or fury in marital, parent-children, or student-teacher relationships. As long as the real-self does not approve of the outcomes executed by the pseudo-self, then the relationships can be fixed.

Overall, as one can see, the hypocrite has the opposite disposition in that their pseudo self has the dialogues of faith, but their real self has the disposition of negativity. The dangerous point reveals itself for everyone and for all of us if the real self loses this trait of regret after engaging oneself with evil.

In other words, they may look for the ways to meet with the believers in order to humiliate or mock them. The state of a hypocrite is not temporary but is a permanent state with the devil.

In this case, there is the language that there are human and spirits or demons and the devils to represent this notion of evil embodiment through humans.

Even, one can realize this notion of the interaction of animals with the realms of the devil. For example, the camels followed by some of the devils [35] [36], the incident of the passing donkeys' during the prayers or rituals [7] or the case of Omar visiting Damascus [37] and riding on a horse can be some examples.

When one reviews the rituals of taking refuge in God, the person chooses the side of God by taking refuge and at the same time, puts the devil on another pole to be away from or distanced from its evil. In some of the discourses of mysticism, there are depictions of the devil. I think some of these statements are expressed in some spiritual states of blindness. The person may not be aware of what they are saying in their conscious or awake state of mind or heart. These interpretations if taken literally can cause major problems with the clear teachings of the religion and mislead many in their creed. Actually, it did. As one can see the projection of these interpretations in traditional eastern religions and also in some of the groups which claim to be under the umbrella of religion but espouse clearly opposing views in their creed that contradict with the clear teachings.

From another perspective, an emphasis in this case can also possibly reveal their real identity. Sometimes, if they are hiding their real identity with something superficial, too much emphasis on this light, thin, and superficial curtain can possibly tear it. Emphasis removes the doubt. The process of removing the doubts entail investigation, inquiry, and analysis. If this process is applied, then their real identity would be revealed.

One of the biggest, most painful positions is to taste a blessing and then to lose it. Since the person knows that blessing and has experienced and tasted it, now without this habit, the person can be in real bitterness and a distressed state. Especially, if the person had some ingredients of faith as the biggest blessing, then the person can be in the highest state of depression in its loss. This in itself can make the person in multiple darkness. Therefore, the highest and expected state is to embody the full state of faith all of the time with beautification in order to remove all of the black points of darkness and to form a continuous and uninterrupted line of faith.

Yes, faith is the biggest blessing for existence. One second or less time of the state of negativity can put the person in very deep and devastating states of darkness.

When a car is ignited with a key or a button, then with a huge initial power of ignition, the car starts and gets going. Faith in a person can be similar to this initial ignition as mentioned with the light or fire. Once it enters, then the person can keep going and speed up quickly or slowly depending on the person in one's relationship with God, increasing one's faith. One can imagine a car starting and stopping, how displeasing it is. The car does not move although it may make some noise. In this case, when the person does not ignite their systems or if there is a problem in the alternator system in car terms, then the car may stop. This can be similar to the expected change or alternation in one's life when the faith enters into one's heart and mind. If there is a problem in this expected change in one's life, then, the person may not embody the faith.

In this perspective, a denier is different than a non-believer. The denier does not have an opportunity to be exposed to the lights of faith because they may not be around the believers. Therefore, if a denier does not have a substantiated prejudice, as soon as they are exposed to the lights of faith as the initial ignition, then they may not leave their state of faith as compared to the hypocrite.

In this regard, a denier after becoming a believer can appreciate all of the states of faith because of the full awareness of contrasting all of the agents of darkness with light, disbelief with faith. In other words, when a non-believer is in persistent heedlessness for the routine practices of faith called negligence, then they may not realize and appreciate the golden life vests of faith. On the other hand, when a denier comes from hunger, poverty, destitution of faith, then this person fully realizes, embodies, and enjoys all of the transforming effects of faith. Yet here the case is full submission with humbleness and humility with open-mindedness and without any prejudice against these golden teachings.

Sometimes there can be a special type of ignition given by God.

In this perspective, one can realize that faith is the guidance. Yet, they made a choice with their own free will not to invest in it similar to a business transaction.

There is a very vivid description that one's imagination and faculties of emotions can be triggered in order to understand something, then picture it and finally contextualize the meanings and feelings in this very colorful depiction. One should remember that in the depictions of the Scriptures and sayings of the prophets, there are no extravagancies or exaggerations. In literature, when humans use metaphorical language or parables, they like to exaggerate as much as possible to get attention. Especially, with our current times of the novel writing industry, the writers may not have concerns about exaggeration and ungrounded cases due to their main concern of being the best seller on the market. On the other hand, in religion there are teachings.

From another perspective, one can understand the existence of metaphorical and figurative language through parables in scriptures. Among many reasons, one is to expand this vivid depiction to get the attention of imaginative and other faculties of a person. This also shows the possible effects of pictures in a human's mind and emotional faculties. This can be positive or negative.

Sometimes, one's imagination accepts and depicts unusual cases quicker. In other words, one's imagination may tend to reject immediately and rationally accessible cases due to being ordinary or cliché. Therefore, one can see here an interesting case of depicting the inner position of hypocrite.

Sometimes, the language that is directing to the mind and logic does not have the capacity to describe the details of inner dispositions of feelings and emotions. In this case, the figurative and metaphorical language in parables can be closer to explaining these details in emotions and feelings by very vividly depicting their inner faculties and emotions of fear, pessimism, uncertainty, anxiety, stress, darkness, panic, gloominess, nervousness, and uneasiness.

In Arabic language, there are different reasons of using similitude or metaphorical language. Some are to explain the possibility of the reality of the topic of discussion, to identify the discussed case, to identify its quantity, to clarify the case in one's mind, to attract the reader's attention, and to make the reader to focus on the case [38].

Here, another interesting concept is the trend that when a person does not have a pure light, they may benefit from the ones who do have it. Hypocrites on the earth used to benefit from the pure light of the faith and its reflections. As the hypocrites were and are living with the false faith, they have been getting some benefit from this faith. If an evil person sits and hangs around with good people, there will be some good effect on him or her even though they maintain the evilness.

With all the mischief and evil renderings of hypocrites, they are still under the control and allowance of God. Sometimes, a person can become pessimistic or hopeless as one follows the news and watches the mischievous happenings on the earth.

They may have a very false or transient type of success or light in this mischief that causes them to feel happy. Yet, when God removes this pseudo or fake light of joy or happiness due to their mischief, then they are again in their normal and continuous state of darkness of lack of faith and full of mischief renderings.

One can ask: Why was their light gone some time after they had tasted the light or the light of faith? Can they have no light from the beginning? When a person tastes a blessing, there is more pain when the person loses it.

This can be that when they had the fire or light of faith, that they did not maintain the necessary means to keep this fire. Then, it disappeared or vanished over the course of time. When there is a fire for warming up in the woods, someone needs to take the necessary means to maintain it so that it does not disappear. Similarly, faith's existence depends on learning. If they are not present, then one's faith can be endangered [7].

In the darkness, if the people see their friends in their surroundings, they may have some relief, but they cannot see them as well. This induces another type of distress, fear, and uneasiness on the person's psychology.

In language, the examples or similitudes have more power to describe the details and engage feelings and emotions of the person with the content of the message.

Although the hypocrites are a group, in the engagements of conflict, the effect of one person's causing conflict can be equivalent with many occurrences and chain reactions of conflict. In other words, a person making conflict can represent a huge group in the effects of its destruction.

Alternatively, when a person is part of a group, the effect of one person can be like the entire group. This can be something both for good or bad.

They choose to make conflict or mischief, but they are not forced to do it. Sometimes, without their choice, a person can find oneself in the middle of a conflict. This case is different than the one who by choice and will creates the conflict.

Most of the time temptations instigated by the hypocrite can externally look reasonable and give light, yet once one gets involved and touches it, then the person can be destroyed. Therefore at the time of conflict, although the person seems to agree with one side, it is better not to touch but to be passive without being involved [7].

They lit the fire not for the purpose of warming up, but for seeing. They do not have the pure light, light of faith so that they can see and use it as the source of guidance.

As one can see in the previous paragraph, how the same thing can become a source of darkness, conflict, evil, and loss for one group-the hypocrites, can also become the light, source of guidance, goodness, ethical, and triumph for the other group, the people of faith.

One of the most difficult things for the ego is fasting, deprived from food and drink.

As humans are intrinsically not grateful and thankful most of the time, people develop this trait of gratefulness over time by training. This training is achieved mostly when the person is deprived of what they have. This deprivation can come either with shocking losses of the loved ones or items, trials, tests, accidents, illnesses, financial difficulties, divorces, trials of the children, family or friends, etc.

The second way is to train oneself deliberately and consciously through the executions of the free will and free choice for attaining the trait of gratitude. This can be through deliberate prayers, fasting, or charity. For example, in the case of fasting, one deliberately chooses not to eat with their free will in order to appreciate and have gratitude to God for the constant bounties. In charity, one tries to detach oneself and appreciate and have gratitude to God for financial stability.

If one chooses to take and follow the second route, the painful and shocking discourses of the first route can be minimized. Yet, if the person chooses the first route, then with it come the difficulties of these trials and unfortunate outcomes on this earth and in the afterlife.

GALAXIES AND THE PERSON

One day, Danna attended a gathering. There was an attendee who was discussing the galaxies. There was another attended who disagreed with the argument and she emphasized the importance of the self in one's own inner journey rather than the outer journeys of spiritual traveling. The teacher was watching the conversation and said, "Both are important to break the attitude of heedlessness and 'I don't care' for different people. It can also be important for the same person who may be going through different conditions with different spiritual states."

> **IN PRACTICE**
>
> It is important to recognize the different avenues given by God to break our attitudes of unrecognition and unappreciation in our relationships with the Divine. Sometimes, the realization of stars, the moon, and galaxies and sometimes a feeling coming from simple human engagement can help the person to break this heedlessness. A person in different states of spiritual engagement can benefit from each at different times. Different people with different spiritual tastes of engagements can benefit differently from each of the available resources.

Self and the Divine

One can understand that the first position is to realize who you are and what you did. Therefore, in the fields of mysticism it is emphasized constantly that the teaching of knowing yourself can bring a person toward knowledge about God.

The real position of seeking forgiveness from the God can be gained by embodying seeking forgiveness from the God over the course of time. Once the person embodies seeking forgiveness from the God, then this is the real position of going to God, being with God, and pleasing God.

The real position of a believer is to be like a tree bending with the wind and coming back to the original position. From this perspective, resetting oneself constantly and coming back to the original, expected, and natural position of natural constitution through seeking forgiveness from the One, and asking forgiveness from God is the first nature of a believer.

In this perspective, we are constantly being engaged with verbal, physical, and even thought and idea-related engagements throughout the day. Therefore, realizing this disposition is the key.

On the other hand, non-believer or denier, has the stance of 'I don't care'. Or they try to find reasons for all the encounters and be in the modes of argumentation, rejection, ingratitude, heedlessness, distraction, unawareness of one's true self, etc. In this position, a person lives all of their life like this, then at one point when they cannot bear the pains of reality, they get knocked down like a tree, but cannot get up.

A person is weak and is but nothing, composed of flesh, meat, blood, and bones. With all of this nothingness in front of God, claiming to be something, using the words against and outside the realms of respect and etiquette and morals with the Creator of everything, the person can put oneself really in a position of mockery and humiliation.

So, in this perspective, the trials and sicknesses can hit the person to remind them of their own selves and their own realities. These times such as surgery, pain, cancer, death, imprisonment, loss of the attached values such as people's wealth or position, and all evil-seeming incidents can be some of these examples and can hit the person hard.

At these times, like a cold shower, the person can re-evaluate one's position, purpose, and goal in life and can perhaps turn back to God. When others see this person in this calamity, everyone can feel bad for this person as a normal human response. It is also expected that observers of this person take some mindfulness from these incidents for their lives.

But, as soon as God removes this calamity from this person either this person can be appreciative and change their previous life, perspective, and attitude with God… Or the person can forget their difficult times and can go back to the old lifestyle, attitude, and habits.

Or, this person can claim that the medicine, doctors, or something helped to remove the evil that this person was in. With this attitude, this person can give credit to oneself because of their choice.

One should realize both attitudes are the attachments of continuation of the prior same unappreciative behavior of God. But this will not last long because life is short.

In the last category, one can also see people who are in a good life and who have good relationship with God. But when tested with the sustenance, their relationship spoils and these people go into the blame mode.

Change and Reversion or Conversion

In other words, a person who has an experience of religious life, can already have the desire of seeking for the unknown and for the not immediately apparent. Sometimes, piety and dedication in one religion can have disadvantages due to upholding strong group identities and not being open-minded. But overall, a person with a trait of the true concern of fear of the unknown beyond this life with an attitude of humility, sincerity, and open-mindedness would be guided.

Therefore, at a personal level, one should ask and check themselves about this change in daily or spiritual schedules.

Self-Accountability and Religion

True Purification with the Prophets

One should remember that we cannot do and understand how to make purification if do not have purification through the prophets. As humans, we need practical examples in the changing conditions of life. As humans, we are not stable. Every day, at every hour, at every minute, and at every second, our emotions, engagements, and ups and downs change, fluctuate, and oscillate. If we do not have guidance around us from other humans, then it is very difficult to be stable and maintain composure and presence.

In today's time, some of the people forget themselves by indulging either in excessive professional work referred to as workaholics. Some indulge in social life or activism. Some indulge in constant talking or lecturing. Yet, it become a fearful prospect to engage with oneself alone in order to realize this problem of instability. Some people can see others as unstable, but they may not look at themselves.

Some indulge with self-reflection, silence, and nature. Yet, since they do not have the true guidance of openings from the revelations, the prophets, and required constant religious acts of reminders of God through prayers and recitation of the revelations, their self-engagements in solitude can become a delusional illusion.

Some indulge themselves with religious acts very much without much realization of the need of the purpose of the religious acts leading to purification. Purification without religious acts may not have a value. Religious acts without purification is nothing but a balloon filled with air.

With all of these points, if one really reviews the life of the prophets, one can clearly and explicitly see the inseparable perspectives of service, knowledge, and character all with the full embodiment of purification.

Falsehood in Self Purification and Following the Devil

One should clearly realize the people who do self-purification are so disgusting. In other words, the people who constantly engage themselves with their clear, false faultlessness but do not even consider the possibility of a minor fault in themselves but always see others as faulty and wrong are the ones who are disgusting, repulsive, and a sample of the devil.

Source of Negativity and All the Spiritual Diseases Due to Lack of Purification

A person who sees themselves as faultless will not be open to listening to anything.

One should remember that Satan still did not realize this root problem of absence of purification. Presence of purification indicates humility and humbleness of realization of one's mistakes. Satan still thinks he is right. On the other hand, Adam did immediately engage in purification by realizing the mistake he made seeking forgiveness from the One to God. This is the main difference—presence of purification or not.

Purification Leading to Reward

In other words, one can say that the purpose of this life is purification of the ego. One calls this the real purpose. Or, it is the real struggle, striving of the ego.

On the opposite, if one does not engage oneself with this real purpose and with a true process, then all of the efforts can be nullified.

DUAL IDENTITIES

Arlo used to immediately detect the ill feelings in himself towards others. One day, he felt the feelings of jealousy towards some people. He immediately caught it and started the work, struggle, and process of terminating these feelings and transforming them into better and positive ones. Another day, a person came to Arlo and praised him about how great he was. Then, he immediately caught his feelings of conceit, vanity, and arrogance. He then immediately engaged in the self-struggle of terminating them and transforming them into more positive ones. Arlo was really getting tired from these constant struggles of the fight within himself between dual identities.

IN PRACTICE

The purpose of life is the struggle between the pure identity of soul as created by God and raw ego, which is pumped up falsely by Satan and with which we are constantly deceived. The struggle is to train this raw ego. The soul should be decision maker but not the raw ego. The purpose of existence is the life-long struggle between the soul and raw-ego. In this struggle, God is All Merciful. God sent us the scriptures, the Prophets and all the other messengers as guidance and role models for us to define the nature of this struggle and to learn how to win the game of life.

Purification for Children

One should remember that children are in the pure, natural, and innate state of purification.

Yet, when they become adults, they have their own preferences going onto either the path of purification or fury or indication.

At another perspective, even children can have purification before puberty. Yet, there can also be the better ones among children.

In this regard, if our purpose of existence is due to our purification of the ego, then a child void of purification of the ego can be a source of grief and sorrow in this life and in the afterlife.

Therefore, as a mercy, death of this type of child can be a mercy both for the parents and the child themselves. It is a mercy for the parents that they see the sorrow of the absence of purification of the ego in their children with implicit and explicit negativity to God and to the parents in the form of gratitude. It is a mercy for the children that if they die before puberty, then they can be with their parents in the afterlife in Heaven.

When etiquette and morals are gone, purification is gone. When purification is gone, the real purpose of existence is misplaced and terminated.

Purification of Food

One should remember that the type of food that we eat has an effect on us in implementing the process of purification of the ego. There should be constant effort of finding and searching for the food that would be clean, organic, pure, and allowed that would support the establishment of purification in oneself.

SPIRITUAL STATES AND BAKLAVA

Margo used to love baklava, a sweet treat. As she was excelling in her spiritual states, self-discipline, awareness, and mindfulness journey, she appreciated that while she was eating baklava it tasted very good. Later, she was suffering psychologically upon realizing that baklava was mostly unhealthy. It is high in calories with sugary carbohydrates. Margo said to herself, "I need to find treats that are healthy and tasty."

IN PRACTICE

It is really important to be aware and mindful of what one eats. It is not only eating a blessed food but eating healthy and pure food that is important. Keeping the body healthy can make the person more sustainable in one's relationship with God in quality and quantity measures. Therefore, although one may desire to die and meet with God, it is also important to have the intention and goal of having a long, healthy life in this world in order to prolong the sweetness of worship and relationship with God.

DISCUSSION QUESTION

1. What is the relationship between food and worship?

Charity as Purification

One should remember that charity is a word derived from the purification. A lot of times our own attachments to wealth prevent us from implementing the teachings of purification against the spiritual diseases such as attachment to the worldly life as opposite to detachment.

Yet, charity is the form of religious actions that builds in the person the notion and character of detachment from everything especially from the wealth of a person that gives the person the feelings of safety, security, power, and authority towards others.

Collective-Social Accountability and Religion

Certainty in Afterlife

Before starting the steps of the expected belief in the afterlife with certainty, one should review nature and all of creation with a perspective. If one looks at all of the universe, the world, day, night, and all of the excellent system that we are in, there is a determined, set, and running, perfect order and structure. There is a purposeful wisdom in the creation. There is nothing in the universe that is useless, purposeless, and excess. Everything is in perfection both in quantity and quality [39]. All the scientific disciplines such as math, physics, chemistry, biology, engineering, and all others in their expertise and scholarship are the witnesses of this perfection with their discoveries of this perfect order and structure in the universe.

After this brief recapping perspective, it is expected to believe in the afterlife with certainty without any doubt as mentioned in this verse. This can be due to a few reasons [34]:

- Due to the system, structure, and order in the universe that necessitate this reality.
- Due to the perfection in the essence of humans that necessitates this reality.
- Due to the necessity of human internal faculties needing the afterlife that necessitates this reality.

The person should be in constant struggle of reaching to the level of certainty about the afterlife and meeting with God. In other words, the person struggles in one's life to have certainty. There are two important points here. A person should have the desire and goal to reach this certainty about the afterlife. Another point is that the need for having certainty for the afterlife cannot allow any type of doubt or skepticism.

It is interesting to note that one of the missions of the devil is to give doubts about the afterlife.

This can also be evidence that the belief in the afterlife comes with certainty and that it cannot tolerate any skepticism.

Another interesting point is that shows the concept of ignoring and trying to enjoy life although there is some type of doubt, skepticism, that is bothering the person from inside, possibly from their conscience.

No Doubt in Afterlife

It is interesting to note that when God sends the books at different times to different people, their approach was with this word *skepticism*. But the scriptures suggest a treatment of this attitude as well with how and why the Scriptures follow a scientific and rational methodology to establish the authority of authentication.

The certainty about the afterlife is also critical in the application of the ethics of personal, familial, and social relationships [42].

In other words, to implement justice in all personal, family, and social interactions, the more the afterlife is detailed in belief, then the more certainty of afterlife belief will increase.

One can also view the anatomy of a human, the number of bones and their functions, the number of different nerves and their functions, the number of systems constituting different organs, the number of cells constituting these organs, the units in each cell, etc. If one thinks about these systems in a human's physical body, how about the spiritual faculties? The soul, emotions, conscience…etc. Actually, this is more complicated. According to many scholars, the real purpose of a human is the discovery of these complicated spiritual faculties. In this perspective, this adds the real value to the person.

Humans think and reflect. Thinking of death without any afterlife can make the person suffer. The animals do not have future-related concerns or worries. They live in the present time. Therefore, God does not torture the people with worries of the future in their present time in the world by causing them to think and reflect about non-existence after death. If non-existence would be the case, then the person would continuously be suffering in the world, knowing and thinking that this person would be terminated from all her or his loved ones.

Humans have very complex internal spiritual faculties. There are a lot of skills that arise from these faculties. There are a lot of thoughts, reflections, and inclinations from these skills of a person. One can refer to this as the conservation of the spiritual faculties in the afterlife through the conservation laws that we witness in our everyday lives in the world.

There is certainty about the afterlife in religions.

From another perspective, faith, knowing, or certainty can have three stages:

1. by knowledge
2. by senses of vision and hearing, especially
3. by taste, fully

In the first case, for example, a person can hear the suffering of another person such as a sickness or trial. They may feel sad and bad. This is knowing by knowledge or intellect. When the person actually sees this person, this is a higher knowledge by witnessing through the senses. The last case is when the person himself or herself is in this difficulty, suffering, or sickness, then this is called the last stage of full knowledge by experience or tasting it. Some people can call this a full sympathy. Some people can call this full certainty.

The last stage is the experiential stage with knowledge.

In the classical approach, one can call this the deep and comprehensive understanding, the knowledge through reason. The other one is mysticism- the knowledge through experience. Both should be complementary. They do not contradict. However, experience and knowledge are the highest stage of certainty, knowing with certainty. Therefore, the real scholars in the field of religion are always described not as intellectuals but as the people of knowledge with forbearance, fear and abstinence, the real people of experiential knowledge. They know all the regular, legal, and apparent sciences of the Scriptures, sayings of the prophets, deep and comprehensive understanding and others. But they live, implement, and experience this knowledge.

The Purpose of Punishment, Hell, or Accountability

There are traditional scriptural approaches that state a believer of God can end up in punishment, and the purpose of the existence of Hell is for the oppressors, but not for the non-oppressors and grateful ones. In other words, everything can have a primary purpose and goal. Yet, secondary effects do not replace this primary purpose. The primary purpose is that Hell is a punishment for the bad, ungrateful and oppressors of life, at a secondary level the hell is to a help a person on the path of God to check and balance his or her actions of free-will in this life. A sense of accountability with a positive certainty with the possibility of punishment can make a person of God more vigilant and responsible about his or her actions in this life and in front of God so that God can enter this person into paradise with the Divine Grace and Mercy.

The One has created the earth and skies for humans for a primary purpose and goal. Yet, there are other creations of the One such as animals and others who receive benefits from the secondary effects.

Similarly, in an institution such as a hospital, the primary people that can be running the show are doctors. Yet, there are other medical personnel who help and support the doctors in their work. In a university, the primary people that can be running the show are professors. Yet, there are other support staff to help them make the teaching possible.

In this case, the case of some of the believers being punished in Hell temporarily can be one of these secondary effects [7].

In other words, the existence of Hell is not for the believers. Its existence is for the oppressors and ungrateful ones [7].

> *Question:* Why does God prepare a punishment for the creation that God has created?
>
> *Answer:* One of the philosophies can be that it is not really to punish the humans or spirits or demons but to deter and stop their purposeful engagements of evil, oppression, and negativity by reminding them of their accountability and the consequences of their actions. This can form positive fear in order to stop them from evil engagements. Although this may not be the highest level of motivation for doing things in one's relationship with God, yet it still causes the people who are operating at a lower level of a spiritual path to reconsider their actions and choices in life.

In other words, the fear of accountability can stop the crimes executed towards people and in one's relationship with God.

This philosophy is to instill the notion of deterrence for an action with its consequence.

If someone tries to bully another person, if they know the consequences, they may stop doing it.

If someone tries to abuse another person, if they know the consequences, they may stop doing it.

If a group plans to attack another group, if they know the consequences, they may stop doing it.

The notion of deterrence can reflect itself in governmental relationships as well. In other words, kings, sultans, or presidents of a country can have a policy of deterrence by establishing a ministry of defense by forming defense mechanisms to instill fear of deterrence if other countries desire to attack them.

If a person knows the consequences of their choices in one's life and in one's relationship with God, they may reconsider one's disposition and stop one's abusive and oppressive relationship with one's own real self- due to one's lack of recognition, purposefully acting blind, ungrateful, and unappreciative in one's relationship with the Creator.

In a similar sense, it is possible that an oppressor or ungrateful person can experience three levels of punishment in one's life with knowledge of certainty, sensational certainty, and tasteful certainty. These punishments can display in one's life through different trials, tests, difficulties, sicknesses, and fears.

After all of the above knowledge of seeing and tasting different punishments in this life, if the oppressive and ungrateful attitude of a person still chooses the negativity, then their final and continuous abode can be punishment in the afterlife.

On the other hand, the above different levels of difficulties can be the means to increase the level of a believer in their relationship with God.

After all of the above knowledge of seeing and tasting, if the believer still chooses the sin, then their temporal abode can be punishment in the afterlife.

If one thinks the opposite, such as the existence of Hell is to punish people, then God does not really need any means or tools such as Hell to punish the creation that God has created. Yet, the existence of Hell has a purpose and wisdom.

In that sense, the detailed description of Hell is explained in the revelations possibly, to deter and convince the person with their faculties of mind and emotions in order for them to really and carefully reconsider their choice and course of actions.

In a similar sense, the wisdom in the laws of the religion of having an army in a country is to deter the people or groups from any type of aggressive and oppressive action towards them.

In this sense, the laws of religions and scriptures prohibit using the power merely to terminate, kill, and cause chaos on earth. The existence or display of power with preparation is to deter the evil-doers from their possible evil choices.

It is critical to realize that these oppressive and aggressive engagements can come from unexpected directions or perspectives. Yet, as a way of following the means, the person follows the causality, means, and has trust in God after making some preparations and leaves the results to God.

Manifestations of Wisdom and Power: This Life and Afterlife

When we consider the difficulties in the world, they may follow a cyclical process of ease and difficulty. In the afterlife, this ease cycle may not necessarily be the case.

In the afterlife, there is the manifestation of power. The manifestation of philosophy can be secondary. The means or reasons covering the realities may not have substance in the afterlife as compared to the cases in this world. In the life of the world, the manifestation of philosophy, wisdom can be prominent. The means or reasons cover the realities.

In this sense, in the afterlife, both the punishments and the pleasures are personalized. In the world, they can be generalized due to the cover of reasons and means. The punishments or pleasures can have an overall effect and influence.

Afterlife in Detail

One can ask the question: What is the difference between explicit presentation of the details of the afterlife in the revelations and hidden or implicit meanings of the scientific discoveries in the world? Why do the revelations follow the same methodology/method of implicit or hidden renderings for the case of full unseen and unknown possibilities similar to the methodology of hinted and hidden style of mentioning the scientific discoveries in the world?

There are multiple levels of answers and explanations to the above questions.

One is that knowing the details of the afterlife may not be easily achieved through mind, reason, and logic-related renderings. Although there can be some extrapolations for the experts, scholars, or Gnostics, it is really difficult to achieve acquisition of this knowledge of the afterlife fully with its details. Especially, this may be impossible for the general public.

Another reason is that implicit renderings of scientific discoveries sets a goal for humanity to discover what is already available in the world that we are in. Therefore, hinting with encouragement is a key as a style to increase the amazements with self-discoveries of big or small struggles in terminology.

On the other hand, the accessibility of the parameters of the afterlife as another dimension or realm is not accessible fully with the path of mind. Therefore, inductive reasoning of scriptures such as the revelations is critical to tell us what is expected in a realm or dimension that we may not be able to fully experience with our five senses, bodies, and within our parameters of our boundaries in this world.

One can use the given knowledge of the revelations to embody these meanings with one's mind as much as possible. Yet, there can be still some limitations for a full grasp due to the change of parameters, dimension, and realms.

Another important critical point in religions is the pillar to believe in the unseen. In this sense, belief or faith is the step of taking the disposition of submission of oneself in the matters of unseen.

On the contrary, for the case of scientific discoveries in this life, imitation or following something blindly is not desired or considered accurate, authentic, or correct. One should need to understand the logic, the governing principles, and their applications as compared to mere submission in the method of science. This is a fully correct and accurate methodology as established by science.

In fact, submission without understanding in the engagements of science and in this world can induce the notion of taking deities other than God. In other words, understanding, critical thinking, logic, and rationalizing are all critical in scientific matters of methodology and it should be, and it must be. Science is based on experimentation through our senses embedded in different tools, deriving means, and repetition of the confirmed results.

On the other hand, faith requires submission to the unseen matters after one correctly and critically chooses an authentic and truly Godly revealed teaching or religion.

In this sense, an authentic religion as an inductive source of reasoning can give explicit and even logic-related dispositions, especially about the core pillars. In other words, one can expect more explicit dispositions and descriptions if there are matters that our minds may not be fully satisfied with if they are the core principles of the religion.

In this sense, if one reviews the revelations, one of the repeated explicit notions found throughout the entire revelations is oneness of the Creator. Then, the accountability of individuals after death for all choices of humans as people of free will and reason in the matters of appreciation to their Creator and in the matters of justice to their own selves and others follow. All of these notions are explicit teachings of the scriptures and prophets such as the revelations and sayings of the prophets.

In this sense, a person of logic submits oneself to the explicit inductive teachings as given in the revelations and sayings of the prophets as established.

In this sense, there is a difference in the concept of 'submission' in Christian theology and other scriptural approaches as compared to the established explicit teachings of the revelations and sayings of the prophet [43].

In some of these theologies, there is an argument that 'we submit because it is mystical'. Yet, in our case we say that 'we submit because it is logical, and at the same time, there are things beyond our understanding of human boundaries at the interface of seen of this world and unseen of the other'.

In this first case of the word 'mystical', it entails the notion that 'I submit because I don't understand. Therefore, I submit because it is mystical'. Yet, in the latter case of true religion, the notion is 'I submit, or I accept because it is logical'. The above rendering of the other religions can be the root of the problems.

The word mystical in the above case can imply blind following by putting the mind or logic on the side. This approach could actually be super dangerously problematic to be abused and it can be fully open to mistreatment.

Here, I am not talking about the sincere seekers of the truth having faith that there are meanings from everything. The problematic discussion here is about the blind submission of the followers of a religion as has happened in the history and their catastrophic results [40] due to the problematic issues of 'mystical', 'submission', and being obedient.

One is required to follow the critical thinking steps of the mind to carefully analyze and review a religion before they accept or engage themselves with the notion of 'submission'. In this sense, the word 'accept' can replace the word 'submit' due to its negative connotations in the Western societies today about religion, gender, and other relations.

This can be one of the core differences of the methodology/ method at the fundamental level of religion with other religions.

Going back to our discussion, the detailed cases of the afterlife are present in the revelations as compared to prior scriptures sent by God. As the person is expected to have belief with certainty in these matters, the detailing of the afterlife can be increased to give more tools for the person to achieve the level of certainty.

It is interesting to review the historical initial encounters of the Christian world with the revelations and some of the style and content richness and differences compared to prior scriptures. Since they did not recognize and understand these perspectives, some few were inclined to make jokes due to their strong group identities preventing them from going into the content and critically analyzing the differences and similarities. Yet, group identities are always there to motivate the uneducated masses with shows and, unfortunately, then catastrophic results follow as one can witness this often in all of the different parts of history [41] [40].

Explicit Arrogance: Historical Disease

One can ask: Why is there an explicit declaration of a punishment as the outcome of this just accountability? Does the Name or Attribute of God as our Creator imply implicit punishment?

This can show the hope perspective of kindness and gentleness as a loving and caring reminder.

The type of punishment as the deprivation of the Beloved in the afterlife can have a relationship with the preference of the Name and Attribute of God.

Inductive Knowledge and Explicit Punishment

In other words, the deductive type of reasoning and experience in our constant, minutely, and even secondly existence and auto-maintenance of our lives proves, dictates, calls, and shouts with a very loud voice about our Creator. Yet, this person who embodied meanness in their character purposefully, intentionally, and by choice acts as a blind, deaf, hard-hearted person with the attitude of heedlessness, "I don't care" about the reminders of God.

As part of the laws of God, when there is an open and explicit miracle such as the revelations, and if the people still do not believe the Scriptures, and yet maintain their attitude with explicit arrogance, then this requires an explicit and open punishment.

In other words, the inductive type of knowledge given to us openly such as the revelations and the prophets, the sayings of the prophets, and the actions of the prophets, in our constant, minutely, and even secondly existence show, prove, dictate, call, and shout with a very loud voice about God. Therefore, this explicit language can indicate an explicit accountability punishment.

In this case, the angels of punishment ask them as if they had the opportunity of explicit and inductive knowledge from God.

Another example of this rendering of an open claim entailing an open accountability of punishment can be this person who embodied arrogance in their character openly, purposefully, intentionally and by choice challenged and claimed a lie of conceit, arrogance, and vanity. Then, accordingly this person becomes an oppressor, and each oppressor received their explicit accountability.

In other words, the scary and fearful renderings of Hell are not for everyone, but for a certain group- the people of negativity among the humans, but not all humans.

One day, I asked one of my teachers, "How should we explain the revelations about punishment to non-Muslims?" He replied, "Tell them that it is for the bad people, oppressors."

In that sense, it can be important to remind of this methodology of our religion that the existence of punishment is for the evil people. This may look like a simple teaching, yet it is an important part of the theology, especially during our times when theodicy has become popular and people are using any means with the beatification of the devil to leave religion and move towards disbelief.

In other words, the punishment of the afterlife is selective, unlike the evil-seeming punishments of this life. It is individualized. Sometimes, a tribulation can come and affect everyone in this life. Yet, even in this case there is the case of protection of God from the evil-seeming general punishment in this life.

Religion, Experience, and Emotions

The Concern for Ending and Locating Different Emotions

When a person is engaged with a bounty, pleasure, or happiness, one of the feelings that decreases the effect of this happiness is worry and concern about its ending. The bargaining of children desiring to play more than their timed period, and the concern of humans to live longer and not die can be some of the examples of these intrinsic desires of humans.

According to the one approach [34], the desire of humans to not die or their desire for never-ending pleasures are intrinsic emotions given by

God to the people for a purpose. This purpose is to first detect and diagnose this desire and then to channel it to the correct means.

Then, we seek the removal of this pain causing anxiety, worry, and concern for the person. When the person knows that the pleasure and happiness that they are experiencing is not going to end, then the quality and quantity of pleasure is amplified and boosted up.

The feeling of the desire is given to humans by God so that they can use it as a guidance to find a place where the call for this feeling can be satisfied. As one tracks the pathway of this feeling, then it leads the person to the result of the necessity and existence of an endless afterlife. Then, the person can rationalize and fulfill the requirements for being in the position of living an endless life in Heaven.

In this regard, all the emotions and desires are given for a purpose so that they can be placed in their appropriate positions [42] [43]. One should really first know oneself. Knowing oneself requires detecting all of these emotions individually, discretely, and separately. The next step is understanding and analyzing them with their purposes as assigned by God in the person. After all of that, it is important to engage oneself constantly in the struggle of keeping the balance of all of these emotions leading to different mental and emotional states. Yet, the struggle of the person to keep the balance can also be named the trials and tests of life as well.

We can take the example of anger.

Anger is not, by its mere existence, a disease in a person. God made this feeling present so that a person can feel a driving force and be motivated to do something against an injustice. On the other hand, it is given by God in order to reveal a person's reality as a test or trial if they can establish balance in the proper usage of this feeling. Anger can lead to oppression, abuse, and injustice. Yet, positive anger can lead to doing something and standing against injustices and establishing structure.

One can refer to this appropriate, balanced perspective as righteousness, and continuity of balance. Another can call this the truth and reality. Another can define this as the correct fulfillment of being a successor of God on the earth.

Similarly, one can extend a similar approach for other feelings, emotions, or states. These can be in human terms such as arrogance, jealousy, the desire for endless pleasure or life, etc.

Arrogance is the name of a negative emotional state that can lead the person to claim something that they do not possess. This is a negative state of destruction. This becomes especially destructive if one claims it in their relationship with God. Yet, another positive term is having an identity and self as the creation and 'servant of God'. In this regard, the arrogance transforms into the pride of being a 'servant of God'. Then, this embodiment of a person as the 'servant of the One' elevates the person above all fears, anxieties, and worries. It places the person in the states of confidence, trust, submission, and reliance on God and independent of all creation. This is not the negative state of arrogance, but the positive state of not being dependent on anything except God.

Jealousy is the negative state of a desire for others to lose what they have. The jealous person hates others and destroys himself or herself with this destruction. Yet, one can transform this into a feeling of 'belonging to' for some specific lofty bounties. In this case, one can ask God to have this bounty for himself or herself and yet at the same time, ask God to increase for their brother in that specific bounty more than before. This lofty bounty can be acquirement of knowledge, or any means that can lead the person to a good action to please God.

TWO CASES

Julia was looking from the window. While looking out the window, she saw two people. One person was addicted to drugs and trying to terrorize people to get money. Another person was walking and seeing an old woman, wanted to help her with her stuff and carry her bags to the station. Julia was trying to understand these two cases.

IN PRACTICE

External representations reflect internal states. In a human being, there is good, love, humbleness. At the same time, there are evil, anger, and arrogance. The person has a choice, free will, but is accountable for one's decision. The person has a goal on the path to excel in the betterment of oneself. If the person does not practice or exercise following a path, or rituals, then the person can be in duality with the inner struggles of themselves in choosing right or wrong.

A human's inner self is like a huge system of government. If the person has the systems or institutions to govern and implement with law enforcement through rituals, then a healthy government or society is constructed. This is called a self on the journey in practice. Therefore, in the above story, there are two different selves involved in deciding and acting on it.

Heaven and Merit and Compassion of God

The result of Heaven is not due to the acquisition or right of the person, but rather it is due to the merit and compassion of God. If it is a right, then it is expressed as, 'your right is given to you'. Yet, when a person wins a lottery in our worldly means, it is not the right of the person.

In our lives, we try to attract the merit and compassion of God with our deeds and intentions with the primary recognition of God with faith. Then, it is the merit and compassion of God that we try to be from those ones.

In that sense, going to Heaven is not a right but a privilege given by God as a merit and compassion. There are a lot of narratives and stories of the people of piety that indicate that they were given the glad tidings of Heaven with their attraction of the merit and compassion of God due to a simple-looking deed and not due to their lives filled with piety.

Our goal in our lives is to involve ourselves as much as possible with the deeds of religious actions with sincerity to please God so that we can have the compassion and merit of God.

We do not trust in our actions, deeds, or religious actions but we do trust in the Mercy, compassion, and merit of God.

The responsibility of the prophets is reaching out and inviting people to God. This should be with the engagements of giving glad tidings, encouragement, love, and positive reinforcement and inspiration to people. Yes, there is the warning and fear perspective of reaching out. Yet, one of the names of the prophets is 'the one who gives glad tidings'. This can be our dominant method of engagement with people.

In other words, one receives the result of their past and completed engagements.

If someone has faith, it is expected that this person will and should display good actions. Faith necessitates, requires, and embodies in the person the display of good, ethical, and moral actions. On the other hand, some people can display outwardly good, ethical, and moral actions but this does not necessarily indicate the existence of faith. It is possible but not required.

A person of negativity can engage with moral and ethical actions in order to leave a legacy of remembrance of good reputation, fame, and other motivating factors as social activists engage themselves. A person of faith engages himself or herself with good actions to please God regardless of whether or not people see or know about it. In fact, a person of faith with sincerity wants their actions not to be known by people but only to be known by God in order to stress and underline the intention of their engagements. This is only and solely to please God.

According to one perspective, the reason is that most of the time the ethical action and morality are known and agreed upon in a society through the transferred knowledge and experience from one generation to another. This knowledge and experience can be due to the prior scriptures sent by God and also due to the intrinsic, natural constitution qualities of a human being.

Sometimes, when a person is describing something that is impossible and difficult to immediately believe and grasp, they may feel the need to take an oath to emphasize its truth and reality in order to remove any possible doubts from people's minds. Similarly, there is this pledge and assurance about the existence of Heaven as having been prepared marvelously for the believers.

Yet, the word is promoted to the front line to emphasize that

- ▶ Heaven is specifically prepared for believers. Believers are not going to a place that has already been used by others in the past. It is fresh, new, and only and solely prepared for the people of faith. One can remember the experience of living in a newly and freshly built house as compared to a used house with its problems, smells, and repairs.
- ▶ Heaven is owned by the believers, and it is not a rental. In other words, owning something gives someone more pleasure, comfort, and peace of mind than renting or leasing it. The feeling of owning in itself has its own pleasure.

The effect of water on human psychology leading to tranquility, calmness, pleasure, and happiness is indicated in some of the recent fieldworks can have this effect on a person as well [44].

The benefits of different types of water such as well water coming from under the ground and spring water flowing from mountains. The minerals included in water content can increase its benefits as an essential need for humans. One can find these essential benefits in water especially coming naturally from well and spring water unlike filtered waters [45].

In this sense, this can increase the pleasure of scenery for a person whose dwelling is in close vicinity to these water sources. Besides its visual pleasures, different sounds of the flowing water can be orchestrated with multiple arches of flowing water at different speeds. A multitude of water sources can also give more accessibility to different water sources to show abundance, ease, and peace of mind.

On the contrary, sometimes, when something is fully new, unexpected, and unusual, a person can express some type of discomfort or fear with the word 'creepy' or 'strange' in American English colloquial language. In this sense, these words can imply something not previously visited, seen, or encountered; unfamiliar or alien, unusual or surprising in a way that is unsettling or hard to understand, unaccustomed to, or unfamiliar with, causing an unpleasant feeling of fear, or unease [14].

On the other hand, routine can imply something to be monotonous, boring, unstimulating dull, tedious, and repetitious; lacking in variety and interest [14].

One can realize the optimization of the pleasures in Heaven by bringing in both perspectives.

Emotional Memories

There are different theories on memories, recollection of the past experience in the field of cognitive science.

In this case, remembering a pleasure in the past and knowing it will exist in the future can give pleasure, happiness, and comfort for the psychology of the person. The person knows that a pleasure that they have in this world will continue in the afterlife and is not going to end. This feeling and knowledge can in itself give the person hope, motivation, and encouragement to work.

Humans especially are motivated when they know what they will get at the end of their work. If the result is something so high that they cannot imagine it, then this in itself can cause problems in the motivation of the person. Most humans would like to have access to the immediate result of their work either in their imaginations, minds, or some type of experience. Humans are not patient, but they are hasty.

There are a lot of stories among people that allude to this reality. One of them is related in the tale of a shepherd being invited to a feast at a king's or sultan's palace. Among hundreds of different foods available at the feast, the shepherd was not happy and did not feel that he was at a feast. The shepherd was looking for his most valued food that he used to enjoy on rare occasions. This was bread crunches in fresh milk.

Similarly, the ayah can indicate our built-up and expected engagements of pleasure in this world to be carried on to the next world. This is to motivate the person in this life for the expected outcomes in the afterlife.

At another level, when some people die today, people get together to remember this person by sharing some memories. This can be known in popular culture as 'the remembering or recollection of a deceased person, especially one who was popular or respected' [14]. In this sense, the word can indicate this type of collective remembrance of the shared experiences and emotional memories.

In other words, when emotional memories are remembered by the individual, then it has an effect on the person. When the same shared emotional memories are remembered and commemorated collectively, then it can have some amplified effects leading to further pleasure, satisfaction, and happiness.

When a person continues their daily habit, there is an embedded pleasure in this habit. There is the case of the negative and boring perspective of routines as well. Yet, the habits such as going to work daily, working out, daily readings, and other scheduled regular practices can make a person happy.

What will be given in the afterlife will not be exactly the same as what was experienced in the world. This can resolve the issues about the negative side of routines. Although these routines may look alike, they will be different and changing to increase the pleasure of the person with these bounties given by God.

THE REALITY OF MISSING

Elora used to think about all of her past nice memories. She felt much pain longing for them: her old friends, mother, father, brothers, sisters, and cherished places. One day, Elora again remembered all of these nice memories. But now she did not feel pain of longing. She thought and said to herself: "Everything that I miss is temporary. I give them a value as if they are permanent and can benefit me. I think I just miss God who is my Friend regardless of time and place."

IN PRACTICE

It is normal to be saddened by memories, especially of missed good teachers, parents, and friends. But all memories and created beings have limits. Putting too much value on them can be painful and result in not giving the full due to the One who deserves to be missed limitlessly. Compared to all other missed items, God knows and appreciates a person's missing and burning feelings for union with God. These emotions, feelings, thoughts, instances, minutes, or days can elevate the person in front of God vertically. This person can be rewarded immensely in this world and in the afterlife by God.

DISCUSSION QUESTION

1. How can one minimize the effects of pain due to the detachment from loved ones?

Hope and Fear: Heaven and Hell

The existence of both Heaven and Hell has a purpose and wisdom. As humans, we have faculties of mind, intellect, and emotions that need to be fed with hope and optimism. At the same time, we have urges and potentials that need to be maintained and regulated with fear of real and full accountability.

- ▶ Hope keeps the person constantly moving forward toward a goal with meaning and purpose.
- ▶ Fear of accountability keeps the person away from abuse and oppression.
- ▶ In this regard, if hope maintains the quantity, then fear maintains the quality.
- ▶ Hope causes the person to engage in many good deeds.
- ▶ Fear causes the person to reach for sincerity, forbearance, and abstinence with intention.
- ▶ Hope generates continuous action.
- ▶ Forbearance, fear, and abstinence maintain sincerity in intention.
- ▶ Hope fuels entrepreneurship.

- ► Fear motivates sustainability and continuity.
- ► Hope fuels the chivalry, young-manliness.
- ► Fear maintains the wisdom, philosophy.

Realities of Fear, Death, and Hope

When we look at both the philosophical and religious discourses of life and being, there is an anonymous agreement that everything that has a life has a beginning and an end, except God. Therefore, God is not similar to the creation.

Yet, as the name 'man' can indicate, the humans are heedless and forgetful in general and in this case, specifically about the reality of death.

Forgetting death causes the person to increase their attachment to the temporal life with endless expectations.

Therefore, one of the true tests of faith for a person is if they really want to meet God with death.

If not, there is the high possibility of attachment to this life in a person even though the person seems to be very pious and religious.

If a person has the desire to die, this may be for different reasons.

One reason can be their suffering in this world and expecting a better life after death.

Another reason can be one's extreme desire to meet with God.

Another reason can be to leave a good reputation behind among the living with one's death.

In all cases, a true and sincere believer of God is prohibited to end their own life or the lives of others. This is mentioned in the scriptures [10] and [46].

Yet, above all, the possibilities of death can exist at the intentional or expectational levels.

The highest of these intentions is to keep and maintain the desire to meet with God.

Sometimes, life becomes so burdensome with trials and tests that the person may not want to live anymore.

Yet, with all evil-seeming incidents and the ugly-looking face of death, a person of God referred to as a person of faith knows that death and evil-seeming incidents are only the means allowed, permitted, and created by God.

In this sense, they don't get disturbed by current events or waylaid by any incident that instills fear, pessimism, and distraction from achieving their goal as existent beings.

On one side, they try to constantly increase their amazement of faith with certainty through both of the books of God- the revelations and the universe. The universe is another book of God to be read, analyzed, and explored with science through the lenses of faith.

On the other side, the people of faith constantly give hope and breezes of faith to everyone around them suffering from the choking depression of spiritual chaos and darkness, and negativity, especially during the times of fear and uncertainty.

COMMUNICATION WITH THE UNKNOWNS AND UNSEEN

Ivy used to engage with people in different religious traditions. She was really surprised when people were getting scared about the unknowns and unseen, especially related to the ones after death. She really felt bad about them but was not able to do anything except give them some advice about believing in the Creator and practicing the rituals.

IN PRACTICE

Depending on the level of the person, there are really no unknowns and unseen. An advanced person on the path can experience God, angels, the good and evil doers, the authentic versus non-authentic, and all others with certainty. Death is a wrong word according to the spiritual people. Death is only a removal of the barriers for the layman. For a spiritual person, death is nothing newer than having temporary states become permanent stations. In the journey of ascension, the prophet visited different dimensions of unseen and unknowns such as the various conditions and dwelling places of the people after death. One of the lowest states in spiritual advancement is the cognition of the condition of the people in the graveyard.

Negativity and Faith

A person of faith has a different perspective on life than the person of negativity. The person of faith can be in the same place, conditions, and time as the person of negativity. Yet, one can be in torture and the other can be in pleasure.

The person of faith can get the true meaning of everything by correctly relating everything to God. The person of faith knows that everything has a purpose, meaning, and is the servant of God. The person of faith lives a life of Heaven with remembrance of the One, constantly remembering God, the All-Powerful, the All in Control, the All Merciful and the All Caring.

On the other hand, the person of negativity sees everything as chaos, randomness, and purposeless. In this randomness, they get scared by all the different possibilities of evil outcomes. They crack their back under the burden of temptation and fear. Thinking of these possibilities and running to seek solutions to everything from everyone increases the fear in this person. The person of negativity lives a life of Hell in this world with all of those wrong assumptions.

A person of sound mind can ask, "Which path is preferred?" Anyone who has even a sliver of a sound mind would accept that faith is not optional but required both for this world and the afterlife.

Faith leads to planning and preparation. Negativity involves no planning or preparation. A person of faith makes preparation with religious actions. A person of negativity does not value religious actions and views it as unnecessary and a waste of time.

Meaning, Purpose, and Religious Actions

Sometimes, we become confused by the means on the way toward the goal and purpose. When a person is traveling and trying to reach a destination, there can be good and bad scenes on the road. Yet, the purpose of the trip is to reach the destination without stopping and wasting time.

Similarly, different means such as work, family, and other engagements can cause the person to lose the purpose. A person very worried about their financial well-being or other worries can cause that person to lose the main purpose and meaning in life.

Well-being is important. Yet, one should desire to have well-being in order to serve one's purpose and goal in life.

The purpose or goal is to make religious actions to God. Religious actions are the expression of loving God as the way the prophets practiced. Following the prophets in all forms of religious actions and in all forms of life is the expression of love for God and the prophets.

Patience and Reliance (Trust)

One of the philosophies of religious actions is to teach us patience. When we say to each other to 'be patient', this trait is not something learned but it is physically experienced and embodied by a person.

Faith brings the perspective of life to embody patience in oneself. Religious actions help this trait to enter into the person as a character trait with practice.

God opens the different spiritual discoveries with one's engagement of patience. An unexpected difficult encounter with something daily can reveal the person's degree of patience.

In this sense, the level of patience can indicate one's faith. The prophets were the embodiment of patience with calmness and serenity. The prophets had the highest level of faith.

Trust, reliance is the fruit of patience as primarily established with faith and through the religious actions of the person. It is a higher, more positive trait or station that comes to those on a higher level as compared to the level of patience.

A person of patience can realize and know that something is a test or trial even if it is possibly evil-seeming. They show the attitude of patience in this situation.

At a higher level, the person of trust sees everything as positive and as a blessing from God regardless of its outer external cover. At this state, the person is constantly in pleasure as compared to the level of patience. The level of patience can sometimes indicate a painful endurance.

THE PROFESSOR

Mavis used to teach at a college. She felt that some of the students were treating her in a disrespectful way. She said to herself, "I need to be patient." As the semester was getting close to the end, Mavis gained empathy for these students and made good friends with them. After the semester was over, one of the students wrote a reflection about Mavis's class that it was his best class in the college. When she read this, she said to herself, "After every difficulty there is an ease."

IN PRACTICE

It is important to be patient in all different walks of life at all times in life. Husband–wife relationships, student–teacher relationships, parent–children relationships, and friend relationships: all require patience to be successful and to have long life effects. In the above story, Mavis had empathy for her students' not respectful behaviors which helped her actualize and apply patience in her relationship with them. After this self-struggle, as God mentions in the scriptures, after each difficulty there is an ease that rewards the person's self-struggle in the form of patience both in this world with positive results and in the afterlife if the person had a right and good intention.

DISCUSSION QUESTION

1. What is the wisdom of having a difficulty after an ease, and having an ease after a difficulty in circular days destined by God?

Happiness

Eternal happiness can indicate two parts. One can be related to pleasing God. This is the highest level of happiness that one can achieve. When the person gains nearness and proximity to God with the guidance of the prophets, this can fulfill the person in all of one's faculties with happiness.

The other happiness can be present due to the bodily satisfactions. This happiness can be present through awareness of one's pleasures through observation, feelings, senses of dwelling, eating, drinking, or through spousal relationships. The happiness gained through these last three fundamental pleasures depend upon continuity and not upon their ending.

The first type of happiness gained from the proximity and pleasing of God is unarguably clear and does not really need explanation.

The second type of happiness gained through bodily satisfaction can have further elaboration.

When a person knows that they are getting the result of one's work, the person gets more pleasure from the reward. Therefore, the person can maximize the pleasure as the result and reward of one's struggle on the path of God.

In addition, in Heaven, a person knows that the sustenance is not going to end as the person is not going to die. This increases one's pleasure about the blessing given by God. If a person knows the blessings or the sustenance is limited and therefore going to end, then this worry and concern can make the person uneasy and decrease the pleasure that one derives.

The revelations are the pure light- light and guidance for the person. The prophets are the practical guidance. Our emotional states change. We want to be in the company of the virtuous, moral, ethical, and pious people in order to receive the benefit of practical guidance. They show us, as role models, how to practice in the realities of life.

Similarly, a good teacher and a good spouse help the person to receive practical guidance as well. There are a lot of times when a person is on the verge of deciding. Most of the things in life can be hit or miss if there is no clear guidance from a good friend, a good parent, or a good teacher.

The prophets embody the highest level of this practical guidance. Then, other people of God can follow accordingly. Having a spouse in this life can indicate sharing the common and shared pains, pleasures, and goals in this life. For a religious person, the spouses share the same goal for the afterlife as well.

In this sense, having a spouse in the afterlife can also indicate this notion of continuation of sharing and companionship that follows beyond this life. It is not only the physical or bodily engagements in spousal relationships, but also the notion of sharing and pleasure that follows beyond that level of engagement.

One should remember that the real taste is with knowing and increasing the closeness with God, increasing the love for God, and knowledge related to the path of God.

Another example is the immediate accessibility of this blessing of food as compared to other food items. One doesn't need to cook or even cut most of the fruit. As soon as the person picks it from the tree, we can eat, enjoy, and get energy from it. On the other hand, for example, meat requires slaughtering, slicing, seasoning, and cooking while vegetables can also require cooking and slicing. As a side note, for the people of God, there is a tradition in some eastern countries that they eat dry fruit as a way of immediate access of nutrition to save time and to concentrate on their learning and religious actions of God. For that level of people of God, spending time cooking can be considered as wasting time and a distraction. Therefore, they quickly satiate their hunger with some dry fruits or food to move on to their real purpose.

One should remember that in the afterlife, all of the needs can transform themselves to another level or motivation. In this world, the person needs to have a residence, food, drink, and the continuation of generations through reproduction and company for the person during one's lifetime. God has placed a motivational pleasure in all cases of needs so that a person can fulfill these needs for existence.

Yet, in the afterlife, the existence of residence, food, or spouse are not due to their end result. Their existence is due to their pleasures. In other words, this life's secondary reason such as pleasure becomes the primary reason in the afterlife.

NOW I HAVE UNDERSTOOD!

Maya did not understand why she was sometimes in spiritual pain and sometimes not. She was engaging in prayer, chanting, reading the scripture, going to temple, and feeling good; but sometimes when she was not engaged, she was feeling so much pain, detachment, and loneliness. One day, she was traveling on a plane. She was thinking again about the painful moments of detachment, disconnection, loneliness, and physical torture. During her trip, she was constantly engaged in chanting with her beads, reading her scripture, and learning from her sacred prophetic books. She was feeling so happy. She was looking down while walking and not looking around at the people and not engaging with her surroundings. As the moments of happiness continued, she said, "Now I have understood!"

IN PRACTICE

In the above story, Maya was in pain when she was detached from God and not engaged in any type of mental, verbal, or physical ritual. In one of the narrations from the prophets, the highest ranked angel—Gabriel—comes, visits him, and teaches him that the highest level of spiritual pleasure, engagement, and happiness is removing yourself and your ego every time it blocks your spiritual progress and causes pain striving to always be in the state of Union.

Reality of Emotions and Experience in the Relations with the Divine

Religion and Migration-Diaspora

The Reality of Forced Migration: Diaspora

One of the realities that involves the people of faith in their true, just, and ethical stance is their expected and possible destiny of the reality of their forced migration from their lands, homes, countries, and residences. In other words, one of the tests for the people of faith who have been forced to migrate is the challenge of the future of the their faith.

The early Muslims faced these challenges only due to their belief and ethical stance for justice. One can see also similar cases at the time of prophets. One should remember that this is an expected possibility for the people who struggle in this life for the pleasure of God with their faith and ethical stance for justice.

Yet, one should really remember that forced migration is a test and trial that can reveal the person's or group's real disposition with God.

Although the person may know this and expect these outcomes, witnessing this mass forced migration of innocent people- men, children, and women, going through different physical, emotional, and psychological difficulties, stresses, and exertions can make the person spiritually devastated.

Hope

At this point, one can ask a lot of questions such as: "Why is this happening? Is there a way to prevent this? Was there a way to prevent this? What can I do by myself? etc."

As we all live at a real time of presence, we are not responsible for the things that we cannot control in front of God, but we are and can be responsible about what we can do or how we can help to reduce the pain of what the people are going through during these emotional stresses, mental and emotional breakdowns, divorces, separations with teared eyes and broken hearts.

Our initial position is and should be to give hope to the people who are going through different cycles of difficulties. Hope is directly related with God [47].

Hope is directly related with faith, religion, and beautification. Hope is directly related with order, structure, purpose, and the goal of one's existence.

Hopelessness and pessimism are directly related with negativity, chaos, and disunity.

At the times of these breakdowns, giving hope as a teaching as part of the requirement of the faith is critical. Giving hope by helping them through the physical means of financial and physical support are critical as well.

God mentions this reality and absolute truth of being hopeful in the revelations. These realities and absolute truths boost our hope.

God transforms the bad deeds of the people whomever are under these conditions into the form of good deeds.

The second reality of the boosting of the hope is the God will make them enter into Heaven.

The third reality of the boosting of hope is the God has all the absolute and best rewards for everyone's efforts.

Sometimes, when we try to give people hope, they may think that it is not real, but they are only ungrounded thoughts or ideas. It is just making the person feel good. So, here hope is like a placebo drug.

God gives assurance with emphasis as an absolute truth and reality to motivate, encourage, and give hope to the person who is in the depths of difficulties and trials.

The Reality of the Need for Helping and the Diseases of our Hearts

It is important to realize the reality of the need of these people leaving their lands, homes, and countries due to the reasons of forced migration. They need different means of livelihood to survive and adapt spiritually and physically with the new openings as God grants.

In this reality of helping, the people who realize this influx of people should make the utmost effort to help them.

The influx of people coming are referred to as immigrants. The locals are called supporters.

In the efforts of helping as supporters for the people who are immigrants, supporters should be in a natural, happy, and content state while helping these immigrants. There should not be any ill feelings in these engagements of helping efforts.

This engagement of helping immigrants should be in such a state and way that the supporters should make sacrifices and go above and beyond in their helping efforts even if it puts them in difficulty of changing their routine lifestyles.

One should understand that when we are helping each other, our ego often engages in the self-dialogue of selfish attitudes such as: "Why are you helping? Isn't there any other person to help them? Why do we need to destroy our routine? Can't there be any other possibility? I think, these people don't need any help. They can survive on their own."

Above are some examples of the self-dialogue of the selfish and raw ego that one should be aware of. Even if these thoughts come to the person, one should take all of the efforts and means to detach and isolate oneself from these thoughts while seeking forgiveness from the One and asking for help.

THE TEACHER AND HUMBLENESS

One day, Cora visited her teacher. The teacher was giving a lecture and using some harsh words against herself to humiliate her own ego in front of the public. Cora was listening and trying to take a lesson from the lecture for her own self.

IN PRACTICE

The teachers are humans. Although the teachers are spiritually blessed and the students revere them so much, they see and locate themselves at the lowest level in order to not be trapped with spiritual arrogance. Genuine humbleness and humility of the teacher is one of the character traits of a good teacher.

The Nature of the People of Forced for Migration

When we study the revelations about the nature of these immigrants forced into migration, one can realize some of their qualities.

One of their qualities is that they are following the guidelines as established by God and all of the prophets as part of the actions of the prophets. These guidelines when followed can reveal the natural state of a human being referred to as natural constitution. In this sense, these guidelines are pure, natural, and fit in the natural human creation as instructed by God.

In this regard, there were, are, and will be people in societies who want to follow and teach themselves from these natural teachings as instructed by God.

It is interesting to realize that the people who oppress and do the injustice of forcing the people to leave their own habitat accept that these people are the people of justice, fairness, solidarity, objectivity, and purity.

One can also measure the quality of the people in today's forced migrations in Muslim societies. if today's modern immigrants have the same quality of following the natural states of following the revelations and actions of the prophets.

Re-Establishment after the Forced Migration

One should remember that it is important to re-establish oneself as an individual, family, and society after the cases of forced migration. In other words, our life is short. Migration is one of the noble practices that the prophets engaged in and we are willingly or unwillingly following these actions of the prophets with the merit and compassion of God.

Yet, we should at look and prioritize our steps in the re-establishment period in our new lives as immigrants for our new engagements.

It is interesting to realize that after recollecting oneself as an individual, family, or group, there can be an order of steps to follow.

The first is possibly to establish a place of worship in this new habitat or land as one's real and primary purpose of life in their relationship with the Creator through religious actions and other affairs. Yet, in this primary established institution, everyone needs a collective encouragement of remembering God.

An Abundance of reminders and remembrances of God will solve almost all of the spiritual and physical problems with the care, merit, and compassion of God. So, ensuring the institutions to establish this primary and essential existential goal of remembrance of the One in abundant quantity is very, critical.

Without the reminder and remembrance of God, all other efforts will be meaningless, less motivating, and people will not recover from their past, present, and future-related spiritual disturbances, diseases, and worries.

Along with this primary goal of remembrance of the One in abundant quantities in the embodiment of praying through institutions such as places of worship, then other responsibilities can follow.

After these forced migrations things such as, financial institutions, helping others, ensuring justice, ethical behavior, and others are all critical in this new venue of land.

Further Steps of Etiquette and Diplomacy after Re-Establishment

One should remember after the re-establishment, one should use their experience of past difficulties in order not to retaliate but to still maintain justice, fairness, and ethical behavior in their new land.

In any land, and especially in the new land of migration, regardless of the people's beliefs, culture, and system, one should maintain justice, fairness, appreciation, and solidarity with the people.

There is an encouragement by God to be the people of justice and fairness.

One should remember that the people who were the oppressors, helping the oppressors, and forcing the people to leave their habitat, homes, and residence are the ones against justice and fairness.

One should remember that during this influx of forced migrations and re-establishments, there will always be the cases and people who would try to take advantage of these situations and possibly have different and wrong intentions.

Yet, even in this situation, it is important to follow a proper etiquette and diplomacy or protocol.

Innate Potential Powers of Humans

One can understand that God has created humans with potential power of three qualities. One is the potential power of intellect, reasoning, and critical thinking. This is referred to as brainpower.

The second is the potential power of temper, anger, indignation, resentment, and disgruntlement. This is referred to as power of temper.

The third is the potential power of lust, desire, and craving. This is referred to as power of desires.

When these three powers in their potentiality are not balanced in action, then mischief can occur and display in personal, family, and social lives.

When these three potential powers are used in balance with guidance, then they can fulfill the needs of the person, family, and society and please God.

The guidance is with the scriptures, inductive teachings applied in deductive teachings of practice, as exemplified by the role models, prophets, and messengers of God.

Breaking the Natural Divine Promise

In this regard, God gave all humans these three potential powers and qualities. In the universe, and in our interactions with the universe, there are constant signs from God. In these engagements, humans with their free will are expected to implement their natural divine promise that they made with God.

In this regard, using these three powers of potentialities with balance are all in the range of natural engagements and middle way engagements. In this regard, this is a promise of the person with God that in their original creation they were going to fulfill their engagements according to the requirements and natural disposition of their creation. One can call this a covenant or natural promise of the humans with the Divine in terminology.

Yet, when the person engages himself or herself with the extremes of these potential powers, then the person breaks their natural stance of their promise, covenant with God.

The Divine teachings through the scriptures teach and remind us how to be natural, befitting our engagements and choices, according to our factory usage of creation.

Middle Way

When we analyze the teaching of middle way, one can realize that this concept is also present in other religions such as Buddhism, Hinduism, Islām, Christianity, Judaism, and is very apparent in Sikhism and others. One can deduce from here that God sent at different times different prophets, messengers, and leads with the same critical, core, and essential teachings. These common teachings are critical in the establishment and maintenance of personal, familial, and social lives.

The notion of middle way can be defined as the understanding of nothing being extreme in the above mentioned three innate potential powers in an individual.

The extremities can then reflect on group levels of familial, kinship, social and even communal engagements.

The extremities or distancing oneself from middle way can be an explicit and implicit rebellion to the innate natural tendencies of all creation, universe, and ecosystem. These tendencies of extremisms cause the natural social structure and order to break into the ideas and movements of unleashed extremities of anger, lust, and demagogy.

Unleashed anger in personal, familial, and partner relationships can cause the popularized terms of all types of (mental, verbal, and physical) abuse, oppression, and bullying in our modern terms.

Unleashed lust in relationships can cause the popularized terms of obesity, rape, and assault.

Unleashed demagogy in politics, policy-making, and governmental levels can cause wars, killing, position and power struggles.

One can see that although we have these innate potential powers of anger, lust, and intellect, they need guidance to stay on the middle way.

Although all the law enforcements in modern societies are designed to keep the people in middle way by force and fear, the enforcements in religions entail teachings to instill an accountability not only in this world but an accountability by the One, Allah, God, Adonai as referred to as our One and Only Creator. The concept of Karma in Buddhism and Hinduism can indicate the similar concepts of ensuring the middle way of these three innate potential powers of humans to be kept in middle way and balance without abusing, oppressing, and harming others and oneself.

THE SPIRITUAL AND THE SEMI-BUDDHIST SPIRITUAL

One day, there was a spiritual person and a semi-Buddhist spiritual person, and they were good friends. The semi-Buddhist also had teachers from the Buddhist tradition. They argued about whose teacher was better than the other.

IN PRACTICE

A wise religious person tries to avoid religious arguments about the superiority of one's teachers over another. It is always important to respect other traditions if someone is identifying or viewing themselves as "semi" as in the story above. Semi is a term borrowed from physics when the nomenclature is used for example for semi-conductors, half or partial conducting metals. Semi in this case can mean a person following half of the teachings of one path and following the rest from another spiritual path. The arguments of identity chaining the person to specific teachers or schools is not new, unfortunately, along the history of practice. Genuine spiritual people are not trapped in these futile arguments although one can view her or his teacher as the best and the most valuable. As one religious teacher said, "One can claim that his or her teacher or school is the best, but one cannot claim that theirs is the only way."

DISCUSSION QUESTIONS

1. How can one define the concept of "semi" in one's life?
2. Do you encounter people often who see or define themselves as "semi"?
3. What is the advantage and disadvantage of being "semi"?

AN ARGUMENT AT THE TEMPLE

One day, there were two people arguing in the temple. One was an Arab and the other was an Indian. The Arab said, "We should follow the Prophet." The Indian said, "No, that is sunnah muakkadah." Charlie looked at them both, smiling, and said to himself, "They are both saying the same thing but using different terminologies. That is the main problem in our world."

IN PRACTICE

It is really important to have wisdom of understanding of people with their cultural, ethnic, and gender background. In the above story, two people from the same religion are arguing about a religious matter. They mean the same but because they use different words, they think they disagree and argue. In the case of the Arab fellow in the story, he feels that he is qualified to directly access the primary sources related to the practice of the Prophet[3] by quoting the prophet on a religious matter. Whereas the fellow from India follows his teacher and uses a technical term from his school of thought. The Arab fellow does not know this technical term and thinks the other one doesn't know anything. The Indian fellow does not know the source of the quote from the Prophet quoted by the other fellow and thinks the other one equally ignorant.

DISCUSSION QUESTION

1. Is it common to witness people arguing about an issue but they really mean something similar or the same? Why?

ACKNOWLEDGMENTS

I would like to thank all my unnamed teachers, friends, and students for their input, ideas, suggestions, help, and support during and before the preparation of this book.

I would like to thank Ms. Toni Hajdaj, Dr. O.B., Ms. Reyhan and Saadet Tutumlu, Mrs. N. Atasoy, and Ms. Anna Engle for copyediting and proofreading the text.

Lastly, I would like to thank all of my family members for their patience with me during the preparation of this book.

AUTHOR BIO

Dr. Yunus J. Kumek is currently teaching at Harvard Divinity School and also, in sociology department at State University of New York (SUNY) Buffalo State. He has been religious studies coordinator at State University of New York (SUNY) Buffalo State. Before becoming interested in religious studies, Dr. Kumek was doing his doctorate degree in physics at SUNY at Buffalo published academic papers in the areas of quantum physics, and medical physics. He has then decided to engage with the world of social sciences through social anthropology, education, and cultural anthropology in his doctorate studies and later spent a few more years as a research associate in the anthropology department of the same university. Recently, he completed a postdoctoral fellowship at Harvard Divinity school and published books on religious literacy through ethnography and practical mysticism: Sufi journeys of heart and mind. Dr. Kumek, who remains interested in physics—solves physics problems to relax—enjoys different languages, German, Spanish, Arabic, Hebrew, Urdu, and Turkish, especially in his research of scriptural and theological analysis. Dr. Kumek takes great pleasure in classical poetry as well.

INDEX

A
Abrahamic Religions, 158
Acquirement, 19
Alienation, 143
Apocalyptic, 150
Attitude and Religion, 117

B
Belief, 18
Belief & Disbelief, 30

C
Chaos, 31
Checks & Balances, 155
Collective Accountability, 178
Collective Rituals, 144
Conflicts, 91, 152
Conversion, 174
Cosmology, 1

D
Diaspora, 207
Disbelief, 18
Doubts, 117

E
Emotional Memory, 195
Emotions and Religion, 189
Epistemology, 63
Essence, 22

F
Free Choice, 19
Free Will, 19

G
Globalization, 146
Government & Religion, 155
Group, 7
Group Association, 7

H
Holy Spirit, 16
Hope, 207
Human Language and Reductionism, 39
Human Value Systems, 48

I
Identities, 95
Inclination, 19
Intention, 1
Inter-Intra Religious, 91

J
Jesus, 16

L
Layered Authority, 155

M

Method of Religion, 78
Middle Way, 213
Migration, 207

P

Personal Change, 174
Pseudo Self, 165

R

Religion and Migration, 207
Religion & Globalization, 146
Religion & Science, 72
Religious, 159
Religious Action, 202
Religious Adaptation, 123
Religious Cosmology, 1
Religious Epistemology, 63
Revelation, 15

S

Purification, 174
Science & Religion, 9
Secular, 9
Self, 13, 163
Self & the Divine, 172
Social constructs, 48
Soul, 13
Spiritual, 159
Spirituality, 163
Spiritual Disease, 106
Stability, 127
Supplication, 48
Symbolism, 91

T

Theodicy, 130
Times of Confusion, 84

W

Western Philosophy, 65

BIBLIOGRAPHY

[1]	E. Divon, Reaching Beyond the Religious, iUniverse, 2010, p. 162.
[2]	G. L. Schroeder, The Science of God, Simon and Schuster, 2009, p. 256.
[3]	D. C. Matt, God & the Big Bang, Jewish Lights Pub, 1998, p. 200.
[4]	A. Taftazani, Sharhu Taftazani, p. 69.
[5]	Aristotle, Aristotle's Metaphysics.
[6]	Y. J. Kumek, Practical Mysticism: Sufi Journeys of Heart and Mind, Dubuque, Iowa, Kendall Hunt, 2018.
[7]	A. Muslim, Sahih Muslim (translated by Siddiqui, A.), Peace Vision, 1972.
[8]	S. F. Wanza, The Creators Caring Heart, AuthorHouse, 2014, p. 150.
[9]	R. T. Kendall, Just Say Thanks!, Charisma Media, 2005, p. 207.
[10]	SInternational, The Quran, Abul-Qasim Publishing House, 1997.
[11]	Y. Kumek, Etnographic Fields Notes In Boston, Cambridge, 2019.
[12]	U. P. Oxford, "Oxford Dictionaries," 2016. [Online]. Available: http://www.oxforddictionaries.com/us/definition/american_english/. [Accessed 2016].
[13]	J. Polkinghorne, Belief in God in an Age of Science, Yale University Press, 1998, p. 258.
[14]	U. P. Oxford, "Oxford Dictionaries," 2016. [Online]. Available: http://www.oxforddictionaries.com/us/definition/american_english/. [Accessed 2016].
[15]	G. S. Aikenhead, Science Education for Everyday Life Evidence-Based Practice, Teachers College Press, 2006.
[16]	C. B. W. G. Samuel Crook, Ta Diapheronta, Or, Divine Characters, University of Michigan, 1638, p. 634.
[17]	M. Al-Ghazali, Ihya 'Ulum al-Din, Dar al-Fikr, 2004.

[1] Hadith 2704.
[2] Hadith 2705.
[3] Hadith.

[18]	R. A. E. M. E. McCullough, The Psychology of Gratitude, Oxford University, 2004, p. 368.
[19]	S. Abu-Dawud, Sunan Abu Dawud, Riyadh: Darussalam, 2008.
[20]	M. Al-Bukhari, The translation of the meanings of Sahih Al-Bukhari, Kazi Publications, 1986.
[21]	C. Groeschel, Alter Ego, Zondervan, 2013, p. 240.
[22]	M. I. I. Bukhari, Moral Teachings of Islam: Prophetic Traditions from Al-Adab Al-mufrad, Rowman Altamira, 2003.
[23]	U. P. Oxford, "Oxford Dictionaries," 2016. [Online]. Available: http://www.oxforddictionaries.com/us/definition/american_english/say. [Accessed 2016].
[24]	P. P. Kenneth C. Ulmer, Knowing God's Voice, Baker Books, 2011, p. 208.
[25]	B. Tucker, SPIRITUAL ILLNESS, LULU, 2016, p. 18.
[26]	J. Meyer, Closer to God Each Day, Hachette, 2015, p. 182.
[27]	T. Boston, The Doctrine of the Christian Religion: An Illustration With Respect to Faith and Practice, Vol. 02, LULU, p. 277.
[28]	Y. Kumek, Ethnographic Notes from M. Fadil (unpublished), 2019.
[29]	Y. Kumek, Etnographic Field Notes from Sh. Ahmad al-Yamani (unpublished field notes), 2020.
[30]	A. Gilani, Methodology of Prophet Muhammad's Islamic Revolution, the University of Virginia, 1989.
[31]	N. Wakwfield, Solving Problems Before They Become Conflicts, Zondervan Publishing House, 1987, p. 59.
[32]	M. Gopin, Between Eden and Armageddon The Future of World Religions, Violence, and Peacemaking, Oxford University Press, 2002, p. 182.
[33]	P. P. E. Padilla, Theology of Migration in the Abrahamic Religions, Springer Palgrave Macmillan US, 2014, p. 192.
[34]	S. Vahide, The Collection of Light, ihlas nur publication, 2001.
[35]	Al-Hakim, Mustadrak, p. 1/612.
[36]	I. Hibban, As-Sahih, pp. 4/612, 6/411.
[37]	M. Razi, Mafatih al-Ghayb known as al-Tafsir al-Kabir, Cairo: Dar Ibya al-Kutub al-Bahiyya, 1172.
[38]	N. Bolelli, Balagatul Arabiyya, ifav, 2009.
[39]	B. Dembowczyk, Cornerstones, B&H Publishing Group, 2018, p. 27.

[40]	V. Volkan, Killing in the Name of Identity: A Study of Conclicts, Pitchstone Publishing, 2014.
[41]	R. Pellegrini, Identities for Life and Death: can we save us from our toxically storied selves?, AuthorHouse, 2010.
[42]	I. A. H. Gazzali, Ihya Ulum ad-din, Fonts Vitae, 2019.
[43]	M. Al-Ghazzali, Al-Ghazzali on Knowing Yourself and God, Kazi Publications Inc., 2003.
[44]	W. J. Nichols, Blue Mind, Little, Brown, 2014.
[45]	P. E. L. Judy T. Tanner, Springs and Bottled Waters of the World Ancient History, Source, Occurrence, Quality and Use, Springer Berlin Heidelberg, 2012.
[46]	P. D. Miller, The Ten Commandments, Westminster John Knox Press, 2009, p. 221.
[47]	R. H. Cubillos, Faith, Hope, and Love in the Kingdom of God, Pickwick Publications, 2017, p. 300.
[48]	Y. Kumek, Ethnographic Field Notes, 2017.
[49]	Q. Iyad, Ash-Shifa, Madina Press, 2006.
[50]	H. Baghawi, Tafsir al-Baghawi al-musamma Ma'alim al-tanzil, Bayrut: Dar al-Ma'rifah, 1987.
[51]	V. R. N. M. A. J. Kennedy, Think: Critical Thinking About Social Problems, Dubuque, Iowa: Kendall Hunt, 2017.
[52]	S. Critchley, The Book of Dead Philosophers, Melbourne University, 2008.
[53]	A.-M. al-Daylamī, Musnad al-Firdaws (مخطوطة مسند الفردوس), Maktaba Ustadh Doctor Mohammad bin Torkey.
[54]	L. J. (Translator), Aristotle, Metaphysics Lambda, OUP Oxford, 2019.
[55]	M. Tirmizi, Jami At-Tirmizi, Dar-us-Salam, 2007.
[56]	I. Majah, Sunan Ibn-i-Majah, Kitab Bhavan, 2000.
[57]	N. Y. L. B. D. Commission, Laws of the State of New York Volume 1, 1952, p. 1249.

CPSIA information can be obtained
at www.ICGtesting.com
Printed in the USA
LVHW011633190821
695611LV00004B/425